Big Book of Small Quilts

Mary Hickey

Oxmoor House®

Big Book of Small Quilts

from the *For the Love of Quilting* series

©1997 by Mary Hickey and Oxmoor House, Inc.
Book Division of Southern Progress Corporation
P.O. Box 2463, Birmingham, Alabama 35201

Published by Oxmoor House, Inc., and Leisure Arts, Inc.

Library of Congress Catalog Card Number: 96-69031
Hardcover ISBN: 0-8487-1562-4
Softcover ISBN: 0-8487-1563-2
Manufactured in the United States of America
Fourth Printing 2002

Editor-in-Chief: Nancy Fitzpatrick Wyatt
Senior Crafts Editor: Susan Ramey Cleveland
Senior Editor, Editorial Services: Olivia K. Wells
Art Director: James Boone

Big Book of Small Quilts
Editor: Rhonda Richards
Copy Editor: Susan Smith Cheatham
Editorial Assistants: Allison D. Ingram, Wendy Wolford Noah
Associate Art Director: Cynthia R. Cooper
Designer/Illustrator: Emily Albright Parrish
Technical Illustrator: Kelly Davis
Senior Photographer: John O'Hagan
Photo Stylist: Katie Stoddard
Production and Distribution Director: Phillip Lee
Associate Production Manager: Theresa L. Beste

To order additional publications, call 1-800-633-4910.

For more books to enrich your life, visit
oxmoorhouse.com

ig Book of Small Quilts is designed to be a guide and companion for you as you learn how to make small quilts. Use the book for inspiration for new projects and color schemes and for instructions in making unfamiliar shapes and designs.

As you page through the book, observe which color combinations appeal to you. Don't hesitate to plan a project using the color combination of one quilt with the block design of another. Feel free to change the number of blocks or the size of the borders or to adapt the quilts. If you improve the designs in any way, consider yourself an independent artist and a creative genius.

Small quilts with simple shapes are the easiest to make, yet have a humble charm all their own. Their simplicity makes them perfect quick projects. Be aware, though, that the pastime of cutting out little patches of fabric and sewing them back together again is highly addictive. Study the pictures, select a project, scheme with your fabrics, and sew a masterpiece.

Mary Hickey

Contents

The Basics of Quiltmaking

In the following pages you will learn all the basics of general quiltmaking, from fabric selection to quilting techniques. Discover what tools are essential for precision piecing and learn new shortcuts to speed-piecing.

As you page through the book, you'll find that each chapter focuses on a specific quiltmaking technique. You will find instructions for that particular technique in the beginning of the chapter, since that method will apply only to that chapter. The information in the following pages, however, applies to all the quilts.

Many quilts in this book lend themselves to strip-piecing methods. Since rotary cutting is far more accurate than drawing and cutting around templates, the instructions provided in this book are for rotary cutting. We provide templates only for the occasional odd-shaped piece.

Stretch yourself to learn some of these easy techniques. Once mastered, they will greatly improve your accuracy, speed, and enjoyment of the quiltmaking process.

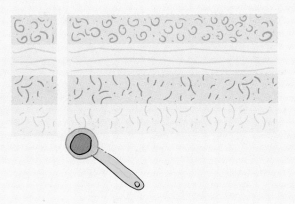

Tools and Equipment

Having the right tools, supplies, and workspace will increase your enjoyment of quilting and improve your accuracy. Purchase the essentials like rotary-cutting equipment and a sewing machine first, and then take some time to accumulate the rest.

Cutting Tools

Rotary cutter: Rotary cutters have done for quilting what microwaves did for cooking. Good rotary-cutting equipment allows you to cut far more rapidly and with greater accuracy than with scissors. Purchase a cutter with a 2" blade for quilting projects. Look at the instructions on the back of the package to see the proper way to hold the brand you bought.

Cutting mat: A good cutting mat is essential for the life of the blade. Look for a cutting mat with a matte surface, not a slick or pebbly one. Purchase one that is at least 18" x 24" and is marked with 1" grid lines.

Cutting rulers: Acrylic cutting rulers are ⅛" thick, which enables you to guide the rotary cutter and protects your fingers from the razor-sharp blade. A 6" x 24" ruler is a good size. Later you may want to add at least three more rulers to your supply: the 6" x 6" square, the BiRangle™ for cutting rectangles and skinny triangles, and a 15" x 15" square. These four rulers, used alone and in combination, will meet most of your needs.

Cutting table: Make your worktable a comfortable height for standing while you cut and work. Most people like a cutting table about 36" high.

Fabric scissors: A fine pair of sharp fabric scissors will become one of your treasured possessions. To keep them in good condition, do not cut anything but fabric with them.

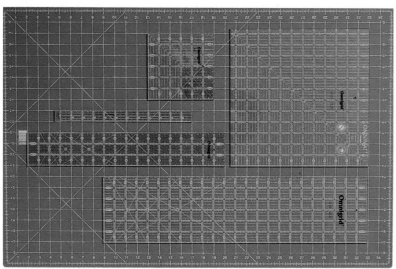

Cutting Rulers

Small Scissors

Fabric Scissors

Paper Scissors

Small scissors: Treat yourself to a pair of small, sharp scissors. Use these for cutting threads, trimming seams, cutting small appliqué shapes, as well as countless other tasks.

Paper scissors: Use an inexpensive pair of large, sharp scissors to cut paper, template plastic, and cardboard—everything except fabric.

Seam ripper: The seam ripper is indispensable for some of us. Since one is never enough, consider buying several and scattering them in spots that will be handy in your hour of need.

Sewing Tools

Sewing machine: Unless you plan to do machine appliqué, a good straight-stitch sewing machine is all you'll need. Be sure to clean and oil your machine regularly. It is important to have a machine that you are comfortable with, one that is your friend and doesn't fight you every step of the way. If you have only a few bobbins for your machine, treat yourself to six or eight more. Wind several with the thread you are using for a quilt so you don't have to stop in the middle of a project to wind bobbins.

Walking foot: If you plan to do your quilting by machine, purchase a walking foot. This will enable the presser foot to move smoothly over the layers of the quilt.

Needles: Replace the needle in your sewing machine regularly. An 80/12 is just right for machine piecing. For handwork, use a size 10 or 11 **sharp** for hand appliqué and a 9 or 10 **between** for hand quilting.

Thread: Use cotton thread for piecing and quilting. You'll find that neutral colors—white, beige, or gray—will work in most instances.

Pins: Steel straight pins with glass or plastic heads and a magnetic pin holder are handy for most pinning jobs. Very thin pins with regular heads are helpful when pinning match points that are difficult to sew. If the pins are extremely thin and you sew slowly, you can leave them in place while machine sewing. Large glass-headed pins or safety pins are essential for basting the layers of the quilt together.

Pressing Tools

Iron: Look for a steam iron that produces plenty of steam.

Plastic squirt bottle: Some fabrics need a spray of water in addition to the steam from the iron.

Walking Foot

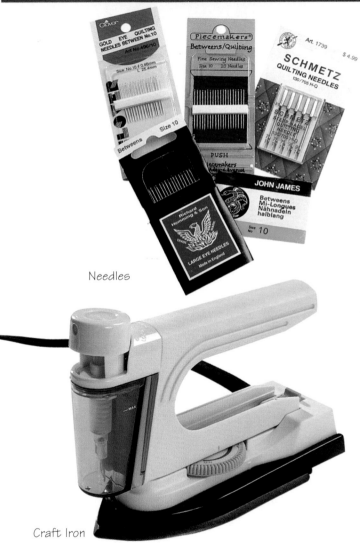
Needles

Craft Iron

Ironing board: An ironing board or large pressing pad at one end of your cutting table will enable you to stand and press at a comfortable height.

Fabric Selection

Quilters have a passion for fabric. Cotton fabrics are softly tactile and infinitely colorful. They beckon to

us from the shops and shelves the way chocolate chip cookies call from the cupboards.

Their colors and textures urge us to touch them, rearrange them, and add and subtract one or two.

Your color choices are probably the single most important factor in determining the success of your quilt.

Color Schemes Based on a Theme Fabric

Try selecting one fabric that will inspire the color scheme for the rest of the quilt. Look for a fabric that has several colors—one that you really like.

Once you have chosen this fabric, stand six feet away from it to see what color it "reads." Avoid a fabric that has only a few tiny dots of the perfect shade, but don't reject one simply because it has a speck of the wrong color.

Vary the size and texture of the prints you select. Mix some larger prints with smaller ones and some linear or geometric prints with some flowery ones.

Bow Ties—Theme Fabric

Scrap or Multicolored Schemes

A single strong color used more than all the rest will often give order and composition to an otherwise wild color scheme. Another way to hold a multicolored quilt together is to use all clear, bright colors— or all grayed colors—or all beige colors (Diagram 2).

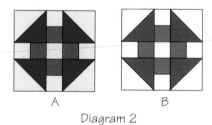

A   B

Diagram 2

Graded Color Schemes

A progression of one color from light to dark or from color to color can add luminosity to your quilts (Diagram 1). Notice the illusion of shimmering in the *Trip Around the World* quilt. The progression of color draws your eye to the quilt and creates a pleasing illusion of light and motion.

Trip Around the World—Graded Color

Churn Dash—Multicolor

Diagram 1

10   Fabric Selection

Color Schemes Taken from the Color Wheel

As you are choosing your fabrics, be sure to place them next to each other. Remember that the colors have a sneaky way of influencing each other or reacting upon one another when they are side by side in a quilt.

Complementary color schemes: Colors that are opposites on the color wheel are complements of each other. *Contrary Wife, Ornery Husband* is a good example of a complementary color scheme, as red and green are opposites on the color wheel.

Warm colors (like yellow and orange) will quickly dominate a design and will advance toward the eye. So unless you want the warms to dominate, it is wise to reduce the amount of warm colors in relation to cool colors (like blue and green), or to use tints and shades of the warms to reduce their impact.

If you have chosen a color and you do not know its complement, try to see its "afterimage." Stare at the fabric for about 60 seconds. Then close your eyes and see what color appears in your mind's eye. Usually you see a tint of the perfect complementary color.

Monochromatic color schemes: Monochromatic quilts are made with tints and shades of one color. To make your monochromatic scheme exciting, use many tints and shades of your color and use a variety of prints to add depth to your design.

Analogous color schemes: Colors that are next to each other on the color wheel are called analogous. They usually make lovely color schemes. The colors in the *Miniature Flying Geese* quilt are all neighbors on the color wheel.

Contrary Wife, Ornery Husband—Complementary

Chubby Checkers—Monochromatic

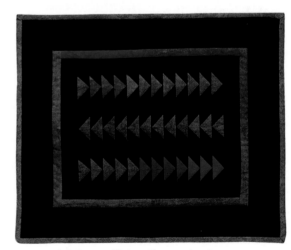

Miniature Flying Geese—Analogous

Prewashing Fabrics

Prewash your fabrics to preshrink them and to wash out the excess dye, chemicals, and sizing added to fabrics in the manufacturing process. Wash darks and lights separately in warm water in your washing machine. Tumble dry in a warm dryer. Press.

Getting Started

Rotary Cutting

By rotary-cutting your fabrics, you can prepare them for piecing much faster and more accurately than by drawing and cutting around templates. A variety of clever strip cutting and piecing techniques has been developed for quilters using rotary cutting. If you are new to rotary equipment, take a few moments to master its use. You will be greatly rewarded for the time you spend. You will be able to stitch many projects you never thought you had the time or patience to create.

Speed Cutting and Piecing Techniques

As you look at the designs in this book, note how often the same set of patches is repeated. Many of these units can be cut in strips, sewn, cut into units, and reassembled for quick and accurate blocks. This saves time and increases your accuracy in two ways: By cutting with a rotary cutter, you can cut many pieces at the same time, eliminating the use of templates. Also, by sewing the long strips together and then cutting the desired shape, you reduce the chance of losing accuracy when you sew or press. For these reasons, I have provided templates only for odd or difficult shapes, such as the tower of a lighthouse.

The First Cut—The Clean-up Cut

The first step in accurate rotary cutting is to trim off the rough edges of your fabric perpendicular to the selvage edges. This cut tidies the edge of your fabric and ensures that the next cut will be exactly perpendicular to the fold.

1. Press your fabric before cutting. Fold the fabric in half with the selvages together. Place it on your mat with the fold toward you and the excess yardage on your left.

2. Place the fold on one of the horizontal grid lines on the mat. Align your 6" x 24" ruler with one of the vertical grid lines, just to the left of the raw edges of the fabric.

3. Cut the fabric with your rotary cutter, rolling it away from you along the edge of the ruler (Diagram 3).

4. After you have made the clean-up cut, you are ready to cut strips. Turn the fabric and mat around so that the clean-up cut is on your left. Align the measurement on the ruler called for in your instructions with the trimmed edge of the fabric. Cut strips across the fabric width from selvage to fold (Diagram 4).

5. As you make additional cuts, line your ruler up with the newly cut edge of the fabric (Diagram 5). Use the grid on your mat to double-check that you are making accurate cuts. Each set of instructions will tell you what size to cut the strips of fabric.

6. After every two or three cuts, make sure your ruler has not slipped and distorted your cuts. Make another clean-up cut if necessary to maintain the proper angle (Diagram 6).

Cutting Shapes

Once you have cut the strips, you can cut simple shapes like squares, rectangles, and triangles from them using a cutting ruler or a template. For some projects you will sew strips together, cut them up, and reassemble them into blocks (Diagram 7).

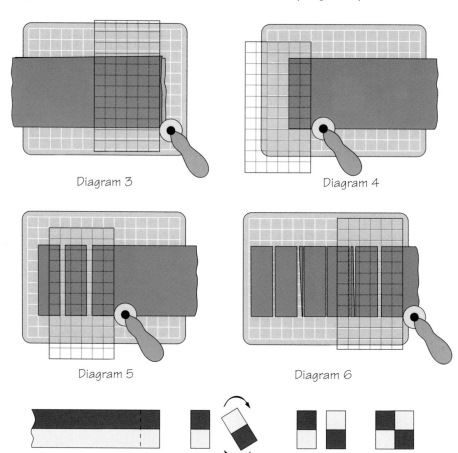

Diagram 3

Diagram 4

Diagram 5

Diagram 6

Diagram 7

Squares and Rectangles

To cut squares and rectangles, start with a strip ½" wider than the finished shape. This allows for a ¼" seam allowance on each side. Place your ruler on the strip and align the desired measurement with the cut end of the strip. Cut across the strip on the right edge of the ruler (Diagram 8).

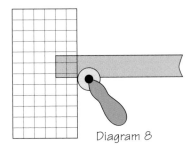

Diagram 8

Triangles

Triangles come in an infinite array of shapes and sizes. Fortunately, as quilters, we have to learn to work with only a few types of triangles:
* two triangles that form a square, called half-square triangles (Diagram 9A).
* four triangles that form a square, called quarter-square triangles (Diagram 9B).
* two triangles that form a rectangle, called half-rectangles (Diagram 9C).
* occasional odd-shaped triangles, called eccentric triangles (Diagram 9D).

In addition, many of the projects in this book make use of a technique called diagonal corners (Diagram 9E).

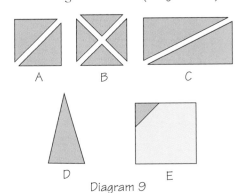

Diagram 9

This is an easy way to add triangles to the corners of squares and rectangles.

The grain lines on triangles must be parallel to the edge of your block. Large side and corner triangles used on the outer edge of diagonally set quilts also require that the straight of grain run parallel to the quilt's edges. This stabilizes the edge of your piece, preventing it from stretching out of shape.

Half-square triangles: If your quilt plan calls for only a few right triangles, the instructions will tell you to cut squares in half diagonally into two triangles (Diagram 10A). Each set of instructions will specify the size of the square to start with. When you cut the square in this manner, the triangles will have the straight of grain on the two short sides and the bias on the long edge (Diagram 10B).

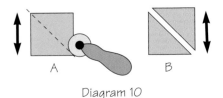

Diagram 10

Quarter-square triangles: Often you will want triangles with the straight of grain on the long side. For a quick way to cut these, cut a square in quarters diagonally, making an X (Diagram 11A). When you cut a square in this way, you will have four triangles with the straight of grain on the long side and the bias on the short sides (Diagram 11B).

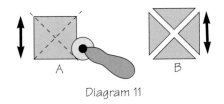

Diagram 11

Side and corner fill-in triangles for diagonal settings: When blocks are set on point, the corners and sides must be filled in with triangles. For the grain lines to be parallel to the edges of the quilt, the corner triangles must be cut from squares cut in half diagonally, and the side triangles must be made

from squares cut in quarters diagonally (Diagram 12).

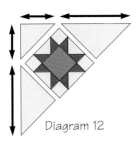

Diagram 12

Half-rectangles: For some quilts you may need only a few long, thin triangles. To make these, cut a rectangle the specified size and then cut it in half diagonally, creating two long, thin triangles (Diagram 13).

A

B

Diagram 13

Eccentric triangles: Occasionally the instructions will tell you to cut a square or rectangle, fold it in half, and then cut diagonally from the bottom cut corner to the top fold (Diagram 14). This will enable you to cut the trees and roofs in several of the quilts.

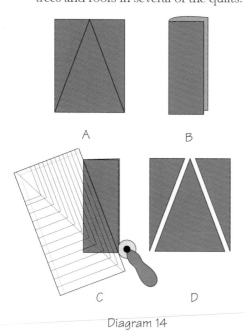

A   B

C   D

Diagram 14

Diagonal corners: Many blocks in this book include triangles at the corners of squares or rectangles. These triangles always begin as squares. With wrong sides facing, fold the corner square in half and press a crease (Diagram 15A). With right sides facing and raw edges aligned, place the square on the base piece. Stitch from corner to corner along the crease (Diagram 15B). Trim the fabric from the diagonal-corner fabric only, leaving a ¼" seam allowance. Press the triangle right side out (Diagram 15C).

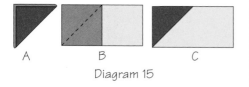

A   B   C

Diagram 15

Sewing the Quilt

The ¼" Seam Allowance

If you learn to master the ¼" seam line, your seams will match up, the points of your triangles will be pointy, the blocks will fit together nicely, and the quilt will lie flat.

Most sewing machines have markings to indicate ¼". Many sewing machines claim to have a presser foot that is ¼" wide. Always check these for accuracy.

To find the ¼" seam line on your machine, make a paper seam guide using the template below. Place the template under the presser foot and lower the needle through the marked seam line. Lower the foot and adjust the paper so that it is exactly parallel with the right edge of the foot. Then place several layers of masking tape on the throat plate next to the right edge of the template (Diagram 16).

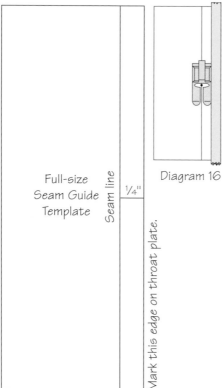

Full-size Seam Guide Template

Seam line

¼"

Mark this edge on throat plate.

Diagram 16

While the template is still in position, measure the presser foot from the needle to the right-hand edge. If it is truly ¼" wide, you can use it as an additional guide. Some machines have a left-to-right adjustment on the needle, allowing the needle to swing to the right to make the edge of the presser foot an accurate guide to use with your tape.

Machine Chain Piecing

Set the stitch length dial on your sewing machine to 12 stitches per inch (written as 2.5 on many machines).

1. By feeding the pairs of fabric shapes through the sewing machine one after another, without clipping the threads between units, you can sew numerous pairs efficiently. This saves both time and thread. Place the pieces that are to be joined with right sides facing. Arrange them in a stack with the side to be sewn on the right.

2. Try to be consistent when you chain-piece. Start with the same edge on each pair and the same color on top. This will help you avoid confusion. Stitch the first seam, but do not lift the presser foot or cut the threads. Feed the next pair of pieces as close as possible to the last pair. Sew all the seams you can at one time in this manner and then remove the chain, as shown in Diagram 17.

3. Take the whole chain of pieces to the ironing board and snip the pairs apart as you press them.

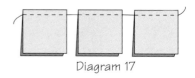

Diagram 17

Putting It All Together

Pinning: Less is better is the general rule for pinning. When you sew small shapes or short seams, you need not pin the pieces unless you are matching points.

When you sew the long seams of a block, begin by pinning the match points (where seam lines or points meet), as shown in Diagram 18. Once these important points are firmly in place, pin the rest of the seam.

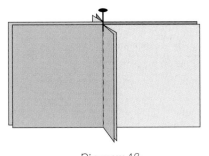

Diagram 18

Pressing: Precise piecing is a combination of accurate cutting and sewing and gentle pressing. Always press a seam before you cross it with another seam. Remember the difference between ironing and pressing. When pressing, you exert a downward pressure on the fabric with a hot iron and then lift the iron up. Quilters let the weight of the iron do the work. In other words, when pressing, don't press down. Ironing, on the other hand, involves a side-to-side sliding motion that you want to avoid to prevent stretching the fabric out of shape.

The traditional rule is to press seams to one side, toward the darker color whenever possible. Side-pressed seams add strength to the quilt. In addition, side-pressed seams allow you to press matching seams in opposite directions. This enables you to butt the seams against each other and more easily match corners and points. Press the seam on the wrong side to fold the seam in the direction you want. Then turn the pieces over and press from the top to make sure the seam is pressed flat without a pleat along the seam line.

Piecing-order diagrams: A piecing-order diagram shows you the steps in which to join the pieces of your block. When a quilter makes a block, she sews small shapes to each other to make larger shapes. For example, when two right half-square triangles are joined, they form a square. When two squares are joined, they form a rectangle (Diagram 19).

These larger shapes, in turn, are sewn together to create the block. By following the piecing-order diagram, you avoid the frustration of having to set in seams and sew around corners. Study the diagrams before you start cutting. You may find that some of the shapes in the blocks can be sewn and pressed first and then cut.

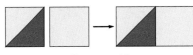

Diagram 19

Pressing

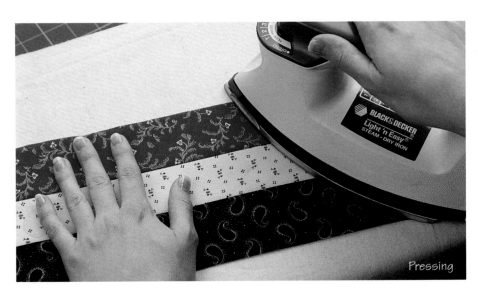

Pressing

Borders

After you have joined the patches to create the blocks and stitched the blocks together to form the quilt top, you may decide to add borders to act as a frame for the design. To measure your quilt for borders, lay it flat on the floor or a table. Measure through the middle of the quilt from top to bottom and then from side to side (not along the outer edges). Cut the borders to these measurements.

It's important to measure border lengths through the center of your quilt, not along the edges, because the edges may have stretched. Stretching gives your quilt a "lettuce leaf" effect and causes you no end of frustration (Diagram 20). It is important that the quilt end up "square," with 90° corners and with opposite sides equal to each other.

Diagram 20

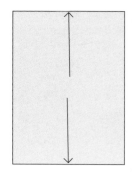 

Diagram 21

Straight-Sewn Corners

1. Measure the length of the quilt through the middle from top to bottom. Trim two of the border strips to that measurement. Sew these strips to the sides of the quilt, easing or stretching as necessary (Diagram 21). By encouraging the quilt to fit the measured strips, your finished quilt will be square with flat borders. This is an important step, so resist the temptation to skip it.

2. To measure the top and bottom borders, measure horizontally across the middle of the quilt, including the side borders and seam allowances (Diagram 22). Cut the borders this length and sew them to the quilt, easing or stretching as necessary. If your quilt will have multiple borders, repeat the order as above, sewing the sides first and then the top and bottom.

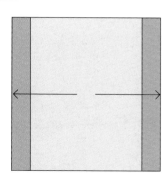 

Diagram 22

Mitered Corners

1. When adding multiple borders that will be mitered, center your border strips on each other and sew them together, creating a striped fabric that can be treated as a unit (Diagram 23). Sewing the strips together makes it easier to match the fabrics on the corners and simplifies sewing the strips to the quilt top.

2. Make a pencil mark exactly ¼" from each corner on the wrong side of the quilt top (Diagram 24).

3. To measure for mitered corners, you will need two sets of dimensions.

Diagram 23

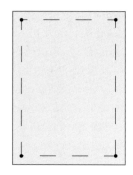

Diagram 24

First, determine the finished size of the quilt, *including the borders,* by measuring through the center. Cut borders about 6" longer than this measurement to allow for seam allowances and ease of matching (Diagram 25).

Next, measure the width and length of the quilt from the pencil mark at one end to the pencil mark at the other end. Use pins to mark the center of each side (Diagram 26A). Mark the center of each set of border strips with pins (Diagram 26B).

4. Center the border strip sets on the sides of the quilt so that the strip sets extend an equal distance beyond each end of the quilt. Match the pins on the border to the corresponding pencil marks on the quilt top and pin, matching the centers, ends, and other important points of matching. Generously pin the rest of the border to the quilt (Diagram 27).

5. Sew the borders to the quilt top using a ¼" seam, starting and ending ¼" from the corners of the quilt and backstitching at both ends (Diagram 28). Add the top and bottom borders in the same manner.

6. With right sides facing, fold the quilt top in half diagonally at one corner so that the adjacent borders are aligned (Diagram 29). Pin.

7. Place a 6" x 24" acrylic ruler with a 45°-angle guideline on top of the fabric, aligning the 45° angle with the long raw edge of the border strips and the edge of the ruler aligned with the fold (Diagram 30). Draw a line along the ruler's edge as shown, from the match point out to the edge of the border strip. Carefully match and pin the corners to form the miters.

8. Sew along the marked line, backstitching at both ends.

9. Trim seam to ¼" and press open (Diagram 31). Repeat to miter each corner.

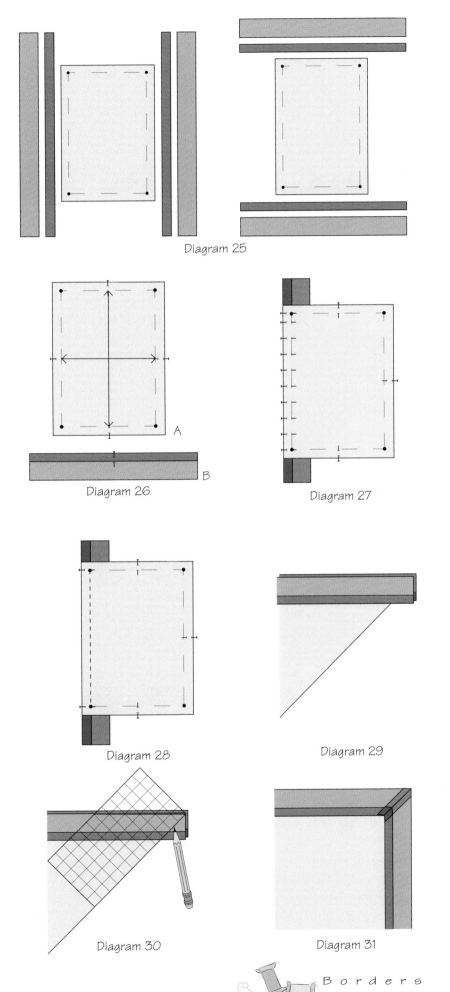

Diagram 25

Diagram 26

Diagram 27

Diagram 28

Diagram 29

Diagram 30

Diagram 31

Quilting

The quilting stitches can be simple outlines of the patches, generous echoes of the shapes, or elaborate patterns that add a completely new dimension of design to the surface. The quilting can be done by hand or by machine. Keep in mind that quilting designs are an essential part of the quilt, so choose them with care.

For many busy quilters, stitching the designs by machine is a satisfying and timesaving alternative to hand quilting. Recent improvements in home sewing machines have solved some of the difficulties of machine quilting. Pick whatever method you prefer and enjoy the magical process of quilting.

Marking the Quilting Lines

Quilters usually prefer to mark the quilting lines on the pieced top before basting the layers. Many beautiful designs are available as stencils from quilt shops. It's best to mark elaborate quilting designs before you sandwich the quilt, when it is easier to trace the quilting design accurately. Straight lines of quilting can usually be marked as you go, and in-the-ditch quilting does not need to be marked at all. As you plan your quilting designs, keep in mind that the layers of fabric in a seam allowance are difficult to hand quilt, so plan your design to avoid stitching across too many seams.

Carefully press the quilt top and trace the quilting designs on it. Many quilters draw the design lightly with a sharp pencil. A mechanical pencil marks nicely. Powdered chalk dispensers, white pencils, and slivers of soap are all useful for marking quilting lines on dark fabrics. A quilt top may also be marked for straight-line quilting with ¼"-wide masking tape after the quilt has been basted. I avoid disappearing-ink markers because the lines have been known to come back years later, especially in humid climates. The lines also become permanent if you accidentally touch them with an iron or otherwise expose them to heat.

Backing

Cut a quilt backing that is at least 2" larger than your quilt top on all sides (Diagram 32). If your quilt is larger than the standard width of fabric, you will have to stitch two or more pieces of fabric together to make the backing. Press this seam open.

Basting

1. Spread the backing wrong side up on a clean, flat surface. Use masking tape to anchor the backing to the surface without stretching the fabric (Diagram 33).
2. Spread the quilt batting over the backing, making sure it covers the entire backing and is smooth. Center the pressed and marked top, right side up, on top of the batting. Make sure that the borders and seam lines are parallel to the edges of the backing (Diagram 33). Pin-baste carefully. For hand quilting, use large straight pins. For machine quilting, use 1" safety pins.

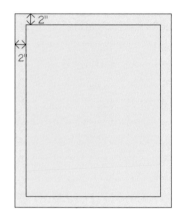

Diagram 32

Diagram 33

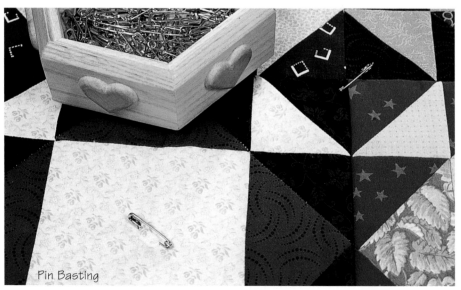

Pin Basting

3. Hand-baste the three layers together, using a long needle and light-colored quilting thread. If you thread your needle without cutting the thread off the spool, you will be able to baste at least one or two long rows without rethreading your needle. Starting at the center of the quilt, use large running stitches to baste across the quilt from side to side and from top to bottom. Continue basting, creating a grid of parallel lines 6"–8" apart (Diagram 34). Complete the basting with a line of careful stitches around the outside edges (Diagram 35). This will keep the edges from raveling while you quilt and also keep the edges aligned when you stitch the binding to the quilt. After the basting is complete, remove the pins.

4. To pin-baste for machine quilting, use 1" safety pins spaced about 2"–4" apart. Start pinning in the center and work toward the outer edges of the quilt. Avoid pinning over your quilting design lines and seam lines where you intend to stitch in-the-ditch.

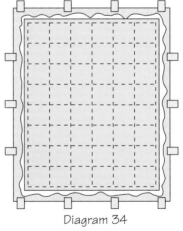

Diagram 34

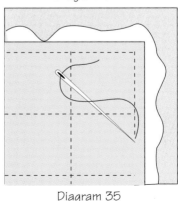

Diagram 35

Hand Quilting

1. Quilting is simply a short running stitch that goes through all three layers of the quilt. Hand-quilt in a frame, in a hoop, on a table top, or on your lap. Use 100% cotton quilting thread. It is thicker and less likely to tangle than regular sewing thread. Beginners usually prefer to use a #7 or larger needle. As you become more familiar with hand quilting, you will find that a smaller (#8, #10, or #12) needle will enable you to take smaller stitches. Wear a thimble with a rim around the top on your middle finger to help you push the needle through the layers.

2. Cut the thread 24" long and tie a small knot. Starting about 1" from where you want the quilting to begin, insert the needle through the top and batting only. Bring the needle up where the quilting will start. Gently tug on the knot until it pops through the quilt top and is caught in the batting (Diagram 36).

3. Insert the needle and push it straight down through all the layers. With your other hand underneath the quilt, feel for the tip of the needle. When you feel the tip pierce the backing, rock the needle to a horizontal position and push the needle back through the quilt

top, pinching a little hill of fabric as you stitch. Rock the needle to a vertical position and take another stitch, loading three or four stitches on the needle (Diagram 37). Pull the needle through, aiming toward yourself as you work. Continue in this way, taking small, even stitches through all layers.

4. To end a line of quilting, make a small knot close to the quilt top and then take one stitch through the top and batting only. Pop the knot through the fabric into the batting (Diagram 38). Clip the thread near the surface of the quilt.

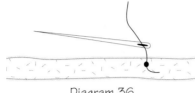

Diagram 36

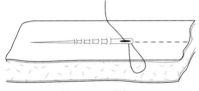

Diagram 37

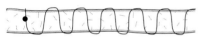

Diagram 38

Hand Quilting

Machine Quilting

Machine quilting is a widely accepted alternative to hand quilting. As quilters find that it takes far more time to quilt a top by hand than it took to piece it, they realize that machine quilting is a practical time-saver.

Plan a quilting design that uses continuous long, straight lines, gentle curves, and few switchbacks or directional changes. In-the-ditch and outline quilting can also be adapted to machine work (Diagram 39). Keep the spacing between quilting lines consistent over the entire quilt. Avoid tight, complex little designs and don't leave large spaces unquilted.

Outline quilting   In-the-ditch quilting

Diagram 39

Select the threads and batting for machine quilting carefully. In the needle, use either a fine 100% cotton silk finish thread or a very fine (.004) high-quality nylon thread made specifically for machine quilting. Thread your bobbin with fine 100% cotton thread.

Many excellent battings (including cotton and wool) are now available that can be quilted with as much as 3"–4" areas left unquilted. Read and follow the instructions that come with the batting you choose.

A walking foot or even-feed foot for your sewing machine will allow the fabrics to move through the machine without shifting. This type of foot is helpful for straight-line and grid quilting and for large, simple curves. Read the machine instruction manual for special tension settings for sewing through thicknesses.

Machine Quilting

Curved designs require free fabric movement under the foot of the sewing machine. This is called free-motion quilting and, with practice, it will allow you to reproduce beautiful hand quilting designs quickly. If you wish to make curved quilting designs with your machine, lower the feed dogs and use a darning foot or a special machine quilting foot. With the feed dogs lowered, the stitch length is determined by the speed with which you run the machine and feed the fabric under the foot. Practice running the machine fairly fast, since this will let you to sew smoother lines of quilting. With free-motion quilting, you do not turn the fabric under the needle. Instead, you move the fabric forward, backward, and side to side.

Make sure your chair is adjusted to a comfortable height. Be patient with yourself. The difference between hand and machine quilting is like the difference between walking and jogging. You can go faster on the machine, but it requires skill and practice.

When all the quilting is completed, remove the basting stitches or pins (except for the stitches around the edges).

Finishing

Making a Sleeve

If you are going to hang your quilt, attach a sleeve or rod pocket to the back before you bind the quilt.

1. Cut an 8½"-long piece of fabric that is the width of your quilt. On each short end, fold over a ½" hem twice. Press and stitch (Diagram 40).

2. Fold the strip in half lengthwise with wrong sides facing and press. With raw edges aligned, machine-baste the top edge of the sleeve to the top edge of your quilt (Diagram 41A). Your quilt should be about 1" wider on both sides. Slipstitch the bottom edge of the sleeve to the backing fabric (Diagram 41B).

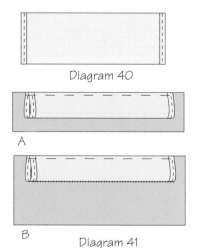

Diagram 40

A

B

Diagram 41

Binding

I prefer to make double-thickness, or French-fold, bias binding. I find that this type of binding wears well and adds a nice finish.

1. Trim the batting and backing even with the quilt top.

2. Place the piece of binding fabric on your mat. Using the 45°-angle line on your large cutting ruler as a guide, cut bias strips 2½" wide. Join the bias strips together end to end using a ¼" seam, as shown in Diagram 42A. Press joining seams open (Diagram 42B). Make a strip that is long enough to go all the way around the quilt plus about 6". Fold the strip in half lengthwise with wrong sides facing and press (Diagram 42C).

3. Align the raw edges of the folded binding with the edge of the quilt top, usually starting along the center right edge. Sew the binding to the quilt top using a ¼" seam. Do not pin the binding to the quilt; instead, smooth it in place about 3" at a time without stretching it. Stop your stitching ¼" from the corner of the quilt and backstitch (Diagram 43).

4. Remove the quilt from the sewing machine. Fold the binding strip to the right at a 45° angle (Diagram 44).

5. Hold the fold down with your finger and fold the rest of the binding back over itself, aligning the raw edge with the second edge to be sewn.

6. Insert a pin from the back of the quilt through the end of your line of stitching ¼" from the end of the quilt (Diagram 45). Start stitching at the spot where the pin comes up through the binding (Diagram 46).

7. Continue around all four sides and corners of your quilt. When all the binding is stitched, turn the quilt over to the back. Fold the binding to the back of the quilt, folding a miter at the corners. To create the miter, press down one side first, and then fold the

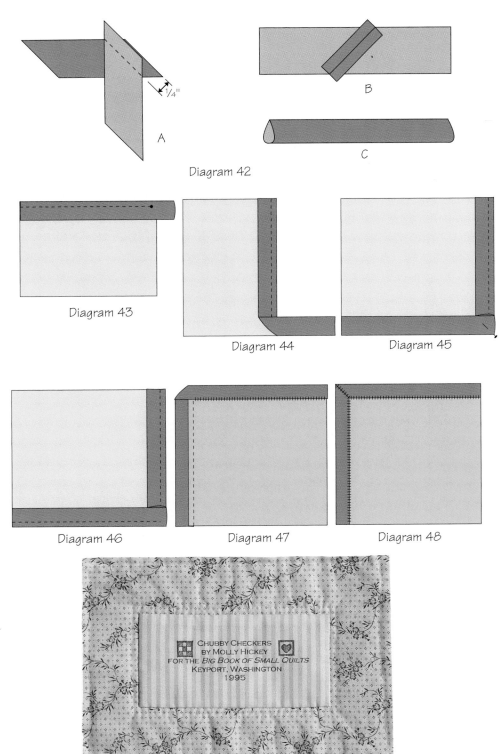

Diagram 42

Diagram 43

Diagram 44

Diagram 45

Diagram 46

Diagram 47

Diagram 48

Label

next side over it (Diagram 47). Complete all four corners this way.

8. Slipstitch the binding to the back of the quilt by hand (Diagram 48).

Labeling

Labeling your quilt is an important finishing touch. Embroider or cross-stitch your name, city, and the date on the back of your quilt. If you have too much information to stitch, you can letter a label with a permanent pen on muslin or even type the information on muslin and stitch it to the back.

Double Irish Chain, page 27.

Quilts Made with Squares and Rectangles

Squares and rectangles are the building blocks of quiltmaking. The patterns formed with these simple shapes are among the most beloved of all quilt designs.

Strip Piecing

Make multiple units more efficiently by stitching strips into a long strip unit and then rotary-cutting it into segments. This saves time and increases your accuracy in two ways. A rotary cutter lets you cut many pieces at the same time and eliminates the use of templates.

1. For a simple nine-patch block, cut the number of strips called for in the quilt instructions. Use your 6" x 24" ruler to make this long cut (Diagram 1). Arrange the strips into two strip units.

2. Stitch strips together for each unit using an exact ¼"-wide seam allowance (Diagram 2).

3. Press seam allowance toward darker fabric.

4. Trim the ends of the strip units and cut into segments in the specified widths for the quilt you are making (Diagram 3).

5. Arrange a stack of the first two segments that you plan to stitch, right sides facing. Pin the match points and stack them so that the same segment is always on the top and the next segment is always on the bottom. For example, if in the first pair you place a dark-light-dark segment on the top and a light-dark-light segment on the bottom, arrange all the pairs the same way.

6. Chain-piece the segments together by feeding them under the presser foot one after another, using a ¼" seam allowance (Diagram 4). Press the new seam allowance.

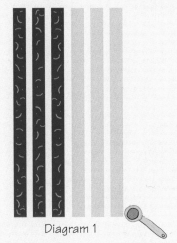

Diagram 1

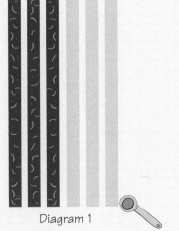

Diagram 2

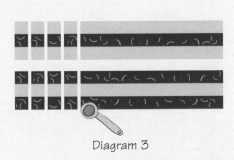

Diagram 3

Diagram 4

Diagram 5

Diagram 6

7. Place the third segment on each unit just sewn. Double-check to make sure you have the third segment on the correct side of the unit. Again pin the match points and stack them next to your machine. Then chain-piece the segments together (Diagram 5).

8. Press nine-patch blocks open (Diagram 6).

Chubby Checkers

Quilt: 30" x 30"
Finished Block Size: 6" square

A plain square is the simplest of all quilt designs. Light blue and white squares
alternate to form the middle of this quilt, while light blue and dark blue make up the border.
To make it easy to keep the lights and darks in the proper place, I suggest you make the
quilt in nine-patch blocks instead of long strip sets.

Materials

1 yard or scraps of whites and muslins
1¼ yards or scraps of light blue fabrics
½ yard or scraps of dark blue fabrics
⅜ yard magenta for hearts and binding
1 yard fabric for backing
1 yard batting

> *Tip:* If you want to speed-piece your blocks but still want a scrappy look, try working with a variety of fabric strips that are about 18" long.

Cutting

From the *whites and muslins,* cut:
• 11 (2½" x 18") strips for Strip Sets A, B, and E.

From the *light blues,* cut:
• 21 (2½" x 18") strips for Strip Sets A, B, C, D, and E.

From the *dark blues,* cut:
• 10 (2½" x 18") strips for Strip Sets C, D, and E.

From the *magenta,* cut:
• 6 (2½") squares for the hearts.

Assembling the Center Blocks

1. Sew strip sets as shown in Strip Set Diagrams A and B:
• 4 of Strip Set A — light blue/white/light blue.
• 3 of Strip Set B — white/light blue/white.
Press all seams toward the light blue.
2. Cut the strip sets into 2½"-wide segments.
3. Join the segments to make 5 blocks as shown in Block 1 Diagram for the center section of the quilt.
4. Join the segments to make 4 blocks as shown in Block 2 Diagram for the center section of the quilt.

Assembling the Border Blocks and Corner Blocks

1. Sew strip sets as shown in Strip Set Diagrams C, D, and E:
• 3 of Strip Set C — dark blue/light blue/dark blue.

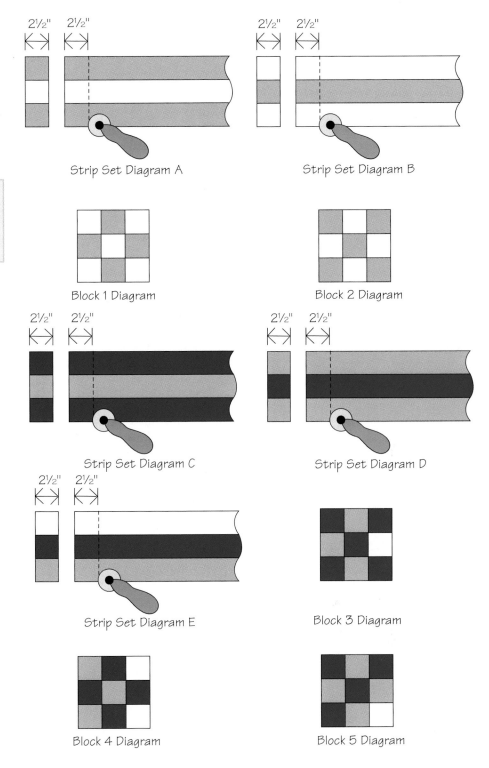

Strip Set Diagram A

Strip Set Diagram B

Block 1 Diagram

Block 2 Diagram

Strip Set Diagram C

Strip Set Diagram D

Strip Set Diagram E

Block 3 Diagram

Block 4 Diagram

Block 5 Diagram

• 3 of Strip Set D — light blue/dark blue/light blue.
• 1 of Strip Set E — white/dark blue/light blue.
Press all seams toward the dark blue.
2. Cut the strip sets into 2½"-wide segments.
3. Join the segments as shown in Block 3 Diagram to make 8 blocks.

4. Join the segments as shown in Block 4 Diagram to make 4 blocks.
5. Join the segments as shown in Block 5 Diagram to make 4 corner blocks.
6. Using Heart Template on page 26, cut out 6 hearts from magenta. Following the instructions for appliqué on page 149, appliqué hearts on the white squares in 6 of the blocks. ┄┄┄┄▶

Assembling the Quilt

1. Join Corner Blocks 5 and Border Blocks 3 and 4 to make rows A and E as shown in *Quilt Top Assembly Diagram.*

2. Join Border Blocks 3 and Center Blocks 1 and 2 to make rows B and D as shown.

3. Join Border Blocks 4 and Center Blocks 1 and 2 to make Row C as shown.

4. Join the rows, alternating them as shown.

Quilting and Finishing

1. Mark the desired quilting designs on the quilt top. The quilt shown has diagonal lines quilted through all the squares and outline quilting around all of the hearts.

2. Layer backing, batting, and quilt top. Baste.

3. Quilt as desired.

4. Referring to the general instructions on page 21, make 120" of magenta bias binding and apply to quilt.

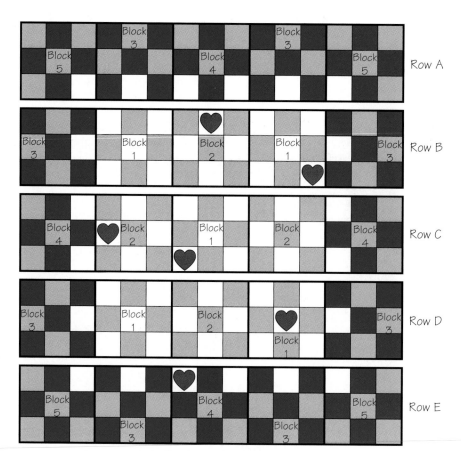

Quilt Top Assembly Diagram

Heart Template

Double Irish Chain

Quilt: 34" x 44"
Finished Block Size: 5" square

Double Irish Chain by Mary Hickey, 1994, Keyport, Washington. Quilted by Hazel Montague.

Many delightful quilts use two different block designs to create a pattern

that is stronger than either block would be alone. A modified checkerboard placed

next to a simple block with only four little checked squares on a blue background make

this lovely pattern. I centered bright bouquets of yellow roses in each of the simple blocks.

Materials

- ½ yard solid yellow
- 1 yard yellow-and-white check
- 1¼ yards blue floral print
- 1⅜ yards fabric for backing
- 1⅜ yards batting
- ⅜ yard yellow print for binding

Cutting

From the *solid yellow*, cut:
- 9 (1½" x 42") strips for Strip Sets A, B, and C.

From the *yellow-and-white check*, cut:
- 4 (1½" x 42") strips for inner border.
- 16 (1½" x 42") strips for Strip Sets A, B, C, and D.

From the *blue floral print*, cut:
- 4 (3¾" x 42") strips for outer border.
- 4 (1½" x 42") strips for Strip Sets A and C.
- 2 (3½" x 42") strips for Strip Set D.
- 18 (3½" x 5½") pieces with roses in the center.

Assembling the Blocks

1. Sew strip sets as shown in *Strip Set Diagrams*:
- 2 of Strip Set A—solid yellow/white check/blue/white check/solid yellow.
- 2 of Strip Set B—white check/solid yellow/white check/solid yellow/white check.
- 1 of Strip Set C—blue/white check/solid yellow/white check/blue.

Press all seam allowances toward the darker fabrics.

2. Referring to *Cutting Diagrams*, cut:
- 34 (1½"-wide) segments from Strip Set A.
- 34 (1½"-wide) segments from Strip Set B.
- 17 (1½"-wide) segments from Strip Set C.

3. Join the segments as shown in *Yellow Block Assembly Diagram* to make 17 yellow blocks.

4. Sew strip sets as shown in *Strip Set Diagram D*:
- 2 of Strip Set D — white check/blue/white check.

Strip Set Diagram A

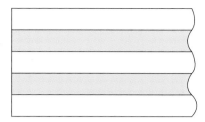

Strip Set Diagram B

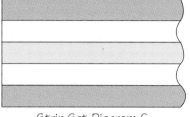

Strip Set Diagram C

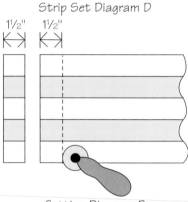

Strip Set Diagram D

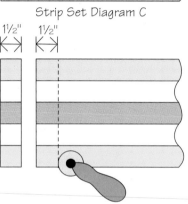

Cutting Diagram A

Cutting Diagram B

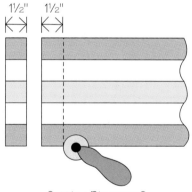
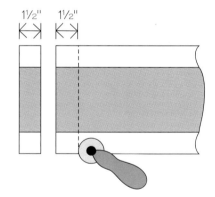

Cutting Diagram C

Cutting Diagram D

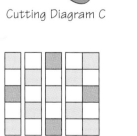

Yellow Block Assembly Diagram

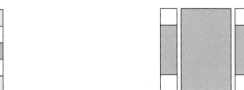

Blue Block Assembly Diagram

Press all seam allowances toward the blue fabric.

5. Cut 36 (1½"-wide) segments from Strip Set D as shown.

6. Join the segments with 3½" x 5½" pieces as shown in *Blue Block Assembly Diagram* to make 18 blue blocks.

Assembling the Quilt

1. Join 2 yellow blocks and 3 blue

2. Measure the width of the quilt, measuring through the middle rather than along the ends. Trim 2 yellow-and-white check inner border strips to this length. Stitch these to the top and bottom of the quilt.

3. Measure the length of the quilt top, measuring through the middle rather than along the sides. Trim 2 blue floral print outer border strips to this length. Stitch these to the sides of the quilt.

4. Measure the width of the quilt, measuring through the middle rather than along the ends. Trim 2 blue floral print outer border strips to this length. Stitch these to the top and bottom of the quilt.

Quilting and Finishing

1. Mark the desired quilting designs on the quilt top. The quilt shown has 2 lines of quilting running diagonally through the yellow blocks and outline quilting around the bouquets in the blue blocks. A curved design is quilted in the outer border.

2. Layer backing, batting, and quilt top. Baste.

3. Quilt as desired.

4. Referring to the general instructions on page 21, make 156" of bias binding and apply to quilt.

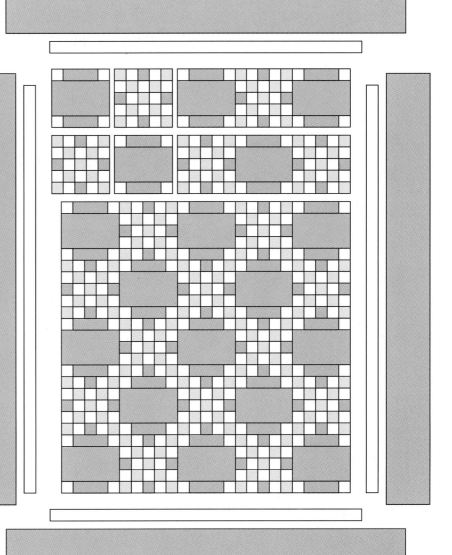

Quilt Top Assembly Diagram

Miniature Santa in the Corner

Quilt: 15" x 15"
Finished Block Size: 2" square

Miniature Santa in the Corner by Mary Hickey, 1994, Keyport, Washington.

Red-clad Santas and dark green squares make up this whimsical mini-quilt.

Tilting the Santas in all directions enhances the design's playfulness. The simple border, made from a striped

red-and-green fabric, only appears to be complex.

Materials

¼ yard novelty Santa fabric (or enough to cut 12 motifs)
⅛ yard muslin for background
¼ yard dark green print for blocks
⅜ yard green striped fabric for borders
½ yard fabric for backing
½ yard batting
¼ yard fabric for binding

Cutting

From the *novelty Santa fabric,* cut:
• 12 (2½") squares, centering the Santas and tilting them as desired. (Quilters call this "fussy cutting.")
From the *muslin,* cut:
• 1 (1½" x 21") strip for Strip Set A.
• 2 (1" x 21") strips for Strip Set B.
From the *dark green print,* cut:
• 1 (1½" x 21") strip for Strip Set B.
• 2 (1" x 21") strips for Strip Set A.
From the *green striped fabric,* cut:
• 4 (3" x 20") border strips.

Assembling the Blocks

1. Sew strip sets as shown in *Strip Set Diagrams:*
• 1 of Strip Set A — green/muslin/green.
• 1 of Strip Set B — muslin/green/muslin.
Press all seams toward the green.
2. Referring to *Cutting Diagrams,* cut:
• 24 (1"-wide) segments from Strip Set A.
• 12 (1½"-wide) segments from Strip Set B.
3. Join the segments to make 13 Cat's in the Corner blocks as shown in *Block Diagram.*

Block Diagram

Assembling the Quilt

1. Join 2 Santa blocks and 3 Cat's in the Corner blocks as shown in *Quilt Top Assembly Diagram.* Make 3 rows.
2. Join 3 Santa blocks and 2 Cat's in the Corner blocks as shown in *Quilt Top Assembly Diagram.* Make 2 rows.
3. Join the rows, alternating them as shown.

Borders

Join the green striped borders to the quilt top, mitering the corners. See the general instructions on page 16 for tips on mitered border construction.

Strip Set Diagram A

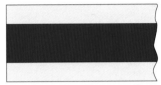

Strip Set Diagram B

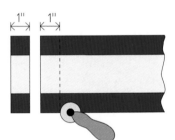

Cutting Diagram A

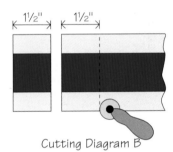

Cutting Diagram B

Quilting and Finishing

1. Mark the desired quilting designs on the quilt top. The quilt shown has a single diagonal line stitched through the Cat's in the Corner blocks in each direction, outline quilting around the Santas, and straight-line quilting in the border.
2. Layer backing, batting, and quilt top. Baste.
3. Quilt as desired.
4. Referring to the general instructions on page 21, make 60" of bias binding and apply to quilt.

Quilt Top Assembly Diagram

 Miniature Santa in the Corner   31

Cat's in the Corner

Quilt: 26½" x 26½"
Finished Block Size: 4" square

Cat's in the Corner by Mary Hickey, 1993, Keyport, Washington. Quilted by Hazel Montague.

The Cat's in the Corner blocks alternate with solid squares of muslin for a simple, cheerful design.

Repeat a motif from your fabric for a quilting design in the set blocks. I used a star.

Materials

¼ yard muslin for Cat's in the Corner blocks

⅜ yard white-on-muslin print for set blocks

⅛ yard red print for Cat's in the Corner blocks

½ yard blue-and-white print for Cat's in the Corner blocks and outer borders

⅛ yard red-and-white stripe for inner border

⅞ yard fabric for backing

⅞ yard batting

¼ yard red print for binding

Cutting

From the *muslin,* cut:
• 1 (2½" x 42") strip for Strip Set A.
• 2 (1½" x 42") strips for Strip Set B.
From the *white-on-muslin print,* cut:
• 12 (4½") squares for set blocks.
From the *red print,* cut:
• 2 (1½" x 42") strips for Strip Set A.
From the *blue-and-white print,* cut:
• 1 (2½" x 42") strip for Strip Set B.
• 4 (3¼" x 42") strips for outer border.
From the *red-and-white stripe,* cut:
• 4 (1¼" x 42") strips for inner border.

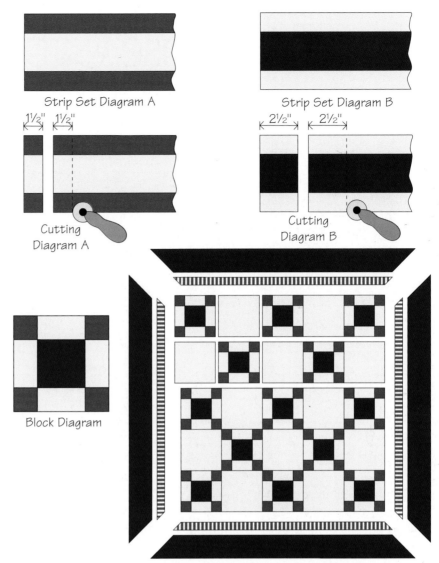

Strip Set Diagram A

1½" 1½"

Cutting Diagram A

Strip Set Diagram B

2½" 2½"

Cutting Diagram B

Block Diagram

Quilt Top Assembly Diagram

Assembling the Blocks

1. Sew strip sets as shown in *Strip Set Diagrams:*
• 1 of Strip Set A—red/muslin/red.
• 1 of Strip Set B—muslin/blue/muslin.
2. Referring to *Cutting Diagrams,* cut:
• 26 (1½"-wide) segments from Strip Set A.
• 13 (2½"-wide) segments from Strip Set B.
3. Join segments to make 13 Cat's in the Corner blocks (*Block Diagram*).

Assembling the Quilt

1. Referring to *Quilt Top Assembly Diagram,* join 3 Cat's in the Corner blocks and 2 muslin print blocks. Make 3 rows.

2. Join 2 Cat's in the Corner blocks and 3 muslin print blocks. Make 2 rows.
3. Join the rows, alternating them as shown.

Borders

1. Sew the red-and-white strips to the quilt top, mitering corners. See the general instructions on page 16 for tips on mitered border construction.
2. Measure the length of the quilt top, measuring through the middle rather than along the sides. Cut 2 blue-and-white print outer border strips to this length. Stitch these to the sides of the quilt.
3. Measure the width of the quilt, measuring through the middle rather than along the ends. Trim 2 blue-and-

white print outer border strips to this length. Stitch these to the top and bottom of the quilt.

Quilting and Finishing

1. Mark the desired quilting designs on the quilt top. The quilt shown has single lines of quilting running diagonally through the Cat's in the Corner blocks and a double-line star in the muslin print blocks. A cable design is quilted in the outer border.
2. Layer backing, batting, and quilt top. Baste.
3. Quilt as desired.
4. Referring to the general instructions on page 21, make 106" of bias binding and apply to quilt.

Rose Cabin

Quilt: 26" x 36"
Finished Block Size: 5" square

This colorful quilt actually contains only four main colors: red, green, blue, and yellow. Each block is made with a red center and four shades of a single color. The areas where the pastels meet create a soft wash of color.

Materials

¼ yard maroon print for block center
¼ yard each of 2 dark rose prints
¼ yard each of 2 light rose prints
¼ yard each of 2 dark green prints
¼ yard each of 2 light green prints
¼ yard each of 2 dark blue prints
¼ yard each of 2 light blue prints
¼ yard each of 2 dark yellow prints
¼ yard each of 2 light yellow prints
¼ yard rose print for inner border
½ yard yellow floral print for outer
  border
⅞ yard fabric for backing
⅞ yard batting
¼ yard fabric for binding

Tip: The quilt shown uses only the lights and darks of one color for each block, with two darks on one side of the block and two lights on the opposite side.

Cutting

From the *maroon print,* cut:
• 1 (1½" x 42") strip. Cut the strip into 10"-long pieces.
From the *dark rose prints,* cut:
• 2 (1½" x 42") strips of each color. Cut the strips into 10"-long pieces.
From the *light rose prints,* cut:
• 3 (1½" x 42") strips of each color. Cut the strips into 10"-long pieces.
From the *dark green prints,* cut:
• 3 (1½" x 42") strips of each color. Cut the strips into 10"-long pieces.
From the *light green prints,* cut:
• 3 (1½" x 42") strips of each color. Cut the strips into 10"-long pieces.
From the *dark blue prints,* cut:
• 3 (1½" x 42") strips of each color. Cut the strips into 10"-long pieces.
From the *light blue prints,* cut:
• 3 (1½" x 42") strips of each color. Cut the strips into 10"-long pieces.
From the *dark yellow prints,* cut:
• 1 (1½" x 42") strip of each color. Cut the strips into 10"-long pieces.

From the *light yellow prints,* cut:
• 1 (1½" x 42") strip of each color. Cut the strips into 10"-long pieces.
From the *rose border print,* cut:
• 4 (1½" x 42") strips for the inner border.
From the *yellow floral print,* cut:
• 4 (3½" x 42") strips for borders.

Assembling the Blocks

1. Select 1 of the 10"-long lights in each color family and stitch it to 1 of the maroon pieces. Press seam away from maroon.
2. Cut the sewn strips into 1½"-wide segments (Diagram 1).
3. Hold 1 sewn pair right side up and with the light square at the top (Diagram 2).
4. With right sides facing, place a strip of the same light fabric on top of the sewn pair. Stitch along the right edge. Press the seams away from the center and trim the strip to the size of the sewn pair (Diagram 3). *Note:* Always sew with the last sewn strip on top (farthest away from you) and the sewn part of the block right side up.
5. Add 2 dark strips in the same way (Diagram 4). Continue to add light and dark strips until the block has 2 rows of lights and 2 rows of darks around the central maroon square (Block Diagram).
6. Make 24 blocks. The quilt shown has 5 rose blocks, 8 green blocks, 8 blue blocks, and 3 yellow blocks.

Assembling the Quilt

1. Arrange the blocks in 6 horizontal rows of 4 blocks each, turning the blocks as shown in the Quilt Top Assembly Diagram.
2. Join the blocks into rows.
3. Join the rows together.

Borders

1. Measure the length of the quilt top, measuring through the middle rather than along the sides. Cut 2 rose print

inner border strips to this length. Stitch these to the sides of the quilt.
2. Measure the width of the quilt, measuring through the middle rather than along the ends. Cut 2 rose print inner border strips to this length. Stitch these to the top and bottom of the quilt.
3. Measure the length of the quilt top, measuring through the middle rather than along the sides. Cut 2 yellow print outer border strips to this length. Stitch these to the sides of the quilt.
4. Measure the width of the quilt, measuring through the middle rather than along the ends. Trim 2 yellow print outer border strips to this length. Stitch these to the top and bottom of the quilt.

Quilting and Finishing

1. Mark the desired quilting designs on the quilt top. The quilt shown has diagonal quilting through the logs and a curved design in the border.
2. Layer backing, batting, and quilt top. Baste.
3. Quilt as desired.
4. Referring to the general instructions on page 21, make 124" of bias binding and apply to quilt.

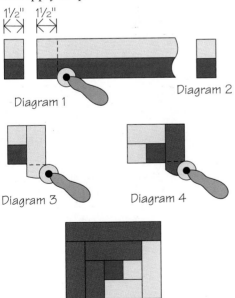

Diagram 1 / Diagram 2 / Diagram 3 / Diagram 4 / Block Diagram

Rose Bud Nine-patch

Quilt: 35½" x 35½"
Finished Block Size: 5" square

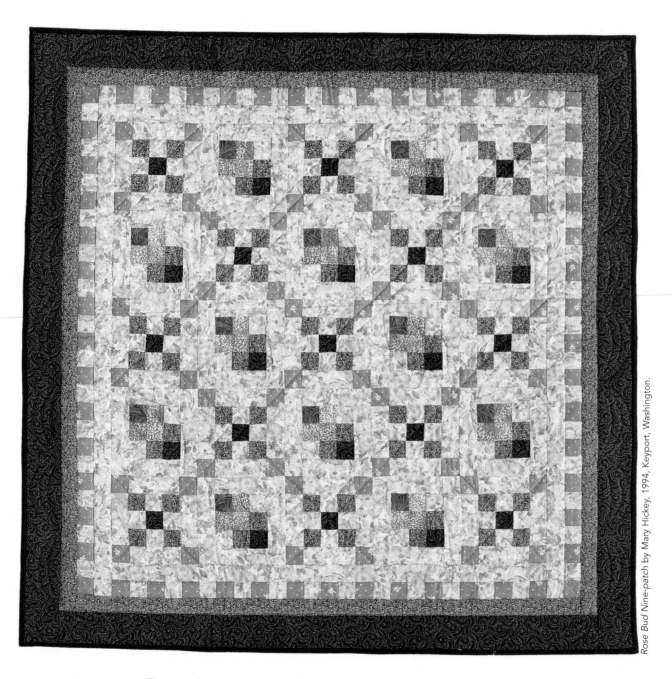

Rose Bud Nine-patch by Mary Hickey, 1994, Keyport, Washington.

Rose-and-green nine-patch blocks create the rose buds in this quilt.

The blossoms are then framed by a Stepping Stone chain. Quilt an oval in each

rose bud to increase the illusion of a flower.

Materials

1½ yards floral print for background and inner border

⅜ yard light green print for Stepping Stone blocks and checked border

½ yard medium green print for rose buds and Stepping Stone blocks

½ yard dark green print for rose buds and Stepping Stone blocks

¼ yard light pink print for rose buds

⅛ yard dark pink print for rose buds

1⅛ yards fabric for backing

1⅛ yards batting

⅜ yard green print for binding

Cutting

From the *floral print*, cut:

• 2 (3½" x 42") strips. Cut 1 strip into 26 (1½" x 3½") pieces for Stepping Stones blocks. Set remaining strip aside for Strip Set A.

• 19 (1½" x 42") strips. From these:
  • Set aside 5 strips for Strip Sets B, C, D, and F.
  • Set aside 4 strips for first border.
  • Set aside 4 strips for second checked border.
  • Cut 4 strips into 24 (1½" x 5½") pieces for Rose Bud blocks.
  • Cut 2 strips into 24 (1½" x 3½") pieces for Rose Bud blocks.

From the *light green print*, cut:

• 2 (1½" x 42") strips for Strip Set A.

• 4 (1½" x 42") strips for second checked border.

From the *medium green print*, cut:

• 4 (1½" x 42") strips for third border.

• 4 (1½" x 42") strips for Strip Sets B, D, and E.

From the *dark green print*, cut:

• 2 (1½" x 42") strips for Strip Sets C and D.

• 4 (2½ x 42") strips for fourth border.

From the *light pink print*, cut:

• 3 (1½" x 42") strips for Strip Sets E and F.

From the *dark pink print*, cut:

• 1 (1½" x 42") strip for Strip Set F.

Assembling the Stepping Stone Blocks

1. Sew Strip Sets as follows:

• 1 of Strip Set A — light green/floral print/light green.

• 1 of Strip Set B — medium green/floral print/medium green.

• 1 of Strip Set C — floral print/dark green/floral print.

Press all seam allowances toward the darker fabrics.

2. Referring to Cutting Diagrams, cut:

• 26 (1½"-wide) segments from Strip Set A.

• 26 (1½"-wide) segments from Strip Set B.

• 13 (1½"-wide) segments from Strip Set C.

3. Join the segments and the 26 (1½" x 3½") floral print pieces to make 13 Stepping Stone blocks, as shown in Stepping Stones Block Diagram.

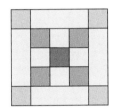

Stepping Stones Block Diagram

Assembling the Rose Bud Blocks

1. Sew strip sets as follows:

• 1 of Strip Set D (dark green/medium green/floral print).

• 1 of Strip Set E (medium green/light pink/light pink).

• 1 of Strip Set F (floral print/light pink/dark pink).

Press all seam allowances toward the darker fabrics.

2. Referring to Cutting Diagrams, cut:

• 12 (1½"-wide) segments from Strip Set D.

• 12 (1½"-wide) segments from Strip Set E.

• 12 (1½"-wide) segments from Strip Set F.

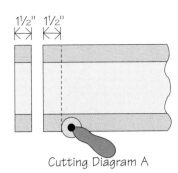

1½" 1½"

Cutting Diagram A

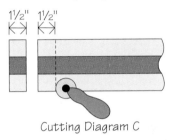

1½" 1½"

Cutting Diagram B

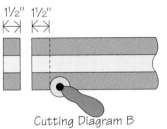

1½" 1½"

Cutting Diagram C

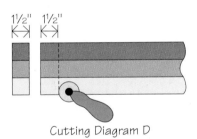

1½" 1½"

Cutting Diagram D

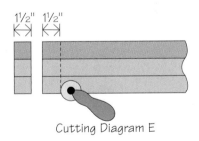

1½" 1½"

Cutting Diagram E

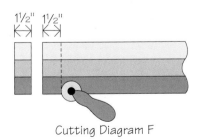

1½" 1½"

Cutting Diagram F

3. Join the segments to make 12 Rose Buds, as shown in *Rose Bud Block Diagram*.

4. Join the 1½" x 3½" floral print pieces to the sides of the Rose Buds.

5. Join the 1½" x 5½" floral print pieces to the tops and bottoms of the Rose Buds to complete the blocks as shown in *Rose Bud Block Diagram*.

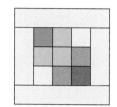

Rose Bud Block Diagram

Assembling the Quilt

1. Join 3 Stepping Stone blocks and 2 Rose Bud blocks. Make 3 rows.

2. Join 2 Stepping Stone blocks and 3 Rose Bud blocks. Make 2 rows.

3. Join rows, alternating them as shown in *Quilt Top Assembly Diagram*.

Borders

1. Measure the length of the quilt top, measuring through the middle rather than along the sides. Cut 2 floral print border strips to this length. Stitch these to the sides of the quilt.

2. Measure the width of the quilt, measuring through the middle rather than along the sides. Cut 2 floral print border strips to this length. Stitch these to the top and bottom of the quilt.

3. Sew the strip set for the border as shown in *Border Cutting Diagram*.

4. Cut the strip set into 1½"-wide segments as shown in *Border Cutting Diagram*.

5. Stitch the segments together to form 2 (27½"-long) side borders containing 13 green checks and 2 (29½"-long) top and bottom borders containing 15 green checks. Use a seam ripper to remove extra squares.

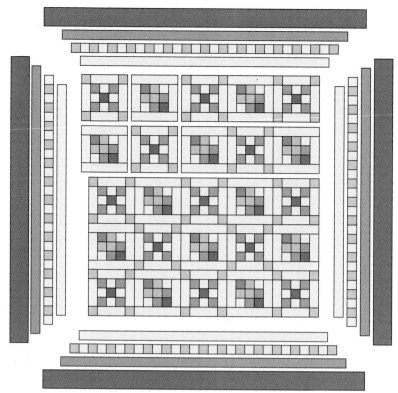

Quilt Top Assembly Diagram

6. Stitch the side checked borders to the quilt top and then top and bottom checked borders.

7. Measure the length of the quilt top, measuring through the middle rather than along the sides. Cut 2 medium green print border strips to this length. Stitch these to the sides of the quilt.

8. Measure the width of the quilt, measuring through the middle rather than along the ends. Trim 2 medium green print border strips to this length. Stitch these to the top and bottom of the quilt.

9. Measure the length of the quilt top, measuring through the middle rather than along the sides. Cut 2 dark green print border strips to this length. Stitch these to the sides of the quilt.

10. Measure the width of the quilt, measuring through the middle rather than along the ends. Trim 2 dark green print border strips to this length. Stitch these to the top and bottom of the quilt.

Quilting and Finishing

1. Mark the desired quilting designs on the quilt top.

2. Layer backing, batting, and quilt top. Baste.

3. Quilt as desired.

4. Referring to the general instructions on page 21, make 142" of bias binding and apply to the quilt.

1½"   1½"

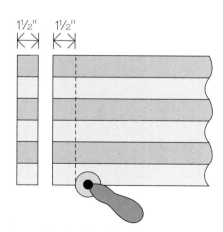

Border Cutting Diagram

Trip Around the World

Quilt: 43" x 43"
Finished Squares: 1½"

Trip Around the World by Mary Hickey, 1994, Keyport, Washington.

Quilters are often teased about buying perfectly good fabric and cutting it up just to sew it back together.

In this quilt I go one step crazier; I sew some seams just to rip them apart.

But by doing this, I make sewing the squares in the proper order so easy that it is almost automatic.

Materials

¼ yard each of 5 shades of green
¼ yard each of 6 shades of rose
½ yard of medium green print for
    inner and outer borders
1½ yards floral stripe for middle border
1½ yards fabric for backing
1½ yards batting
⅜ yard fabric for binding
Seam ripper (Don't panic.)

Cutting

From each of the 5 *green fabrics*, cut:
• 2 (2" x 42") strips.
From each of the 6 *rose fabrics*, cut:
• 2 (2" x 42") strips.
From the *medium green print*, cut:
• 4 (1¼" x 42") strips for inner border.
• 4 (2" x 43") strips for outer border.
• 2 (2" x 42") strips.
From the *floral stripe*, cut:
• Cut 4 (4" x 46") strips for middle
    border.

Making the Rows

1. Using 1 strip of each color, arrange
the 11 strips in the order in which they
will appear in the quilt, from dark
green to light green to light rose to dark
rose. Stitch the arranged strips into a
strip set. Press the seams open. Then
with right sides facing, stitch the long
edges of the strip set together, forming
a tube (Diagram 1).
2. Repeat with the remaining 11 strips
to form a second tube.
3. Lay 1 of the tubes on your mat (you
will have to fold the unit in half to lay
it flat). Carefully cut across the tube at
2" intervals, forming loops (Diagram
2). Repeat with the second tube.

Tip: Stop after every third cut to make
sure your cuts are at a true right angle
with the seams.

4. Use your seam ripper to open 1
loop (Diagram 3). Start next to the
darkest green square and pick the

seam open. Then remove the darkest
green square from the segment
(Diagram 4).
5. Take a second loop and open the
seam between the darkest green and
the second darkest green. Arrange the
second segment so that the darkest
rose is on both sides of the darkest
green. Place the segments with right
sides facing and stitch the darkest rose
of Segment 1 to the darkest green of
Segment 2. You have completed Row 1
(Diagram 5). Repeat for Row 21.
6. Take another loop and open the
seam between green #2 and green #3.
Then remove green #2 from the end

of the segment.
7. Take another loop and open the
seam between green #2 and green #3.
Arrange the segment so that green #1
is on both sides of green #2. Place the
segments with right sides facing and
stitch green #2 to green #1 to complete
Row 2 (Diagram 6). Repeat for Row 20.
8. Repeat this process with each suc-
ceeding shade, always moving to the
next color in the arrangement. Use 2
loops for each row, remembering to
remove 1 square.

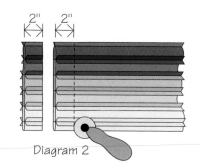

Diagram 1   Diagram 2

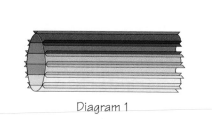

Diagram 3

Segment 1

Diagram 4

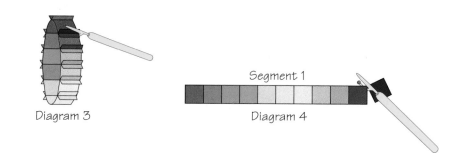

Segment 1   Segment 2   Row 1

Diagram 5

Segment 3   Segment 4   Row 2

Diagram 6

Assembling the Quilt

1. Referring to the *Quilt Top Assembly Diagram*, arrange the rows in the order shown.

2. Stitch the rows in pairs, matching the corners and pressing all seams in 1 direction.

3. Join the pairs of rows together to form the quilt top.

Borders

1. Sew the 3 borders together in strip sets: narrow green/floral stripe/wide green. Stitch the strip sets to the quilt top, mitering the corners. See the general instructions on page 16 for tips on mitered border construction.

Quilting and Finishing

1. Mark the desired quilting designs on the quilt top. The quilt shown has single lines of quilting running diagonally through all the squares. The flowers in the floral stripe are outline-quilted. A curved design is quilted in the outer border.

2. Layer backing, batting, and quilt top. Baste.

3. Quilt as desired.

4. Referring to the general instructions on page 21, make 172" of bias binding and apply to the quilt.

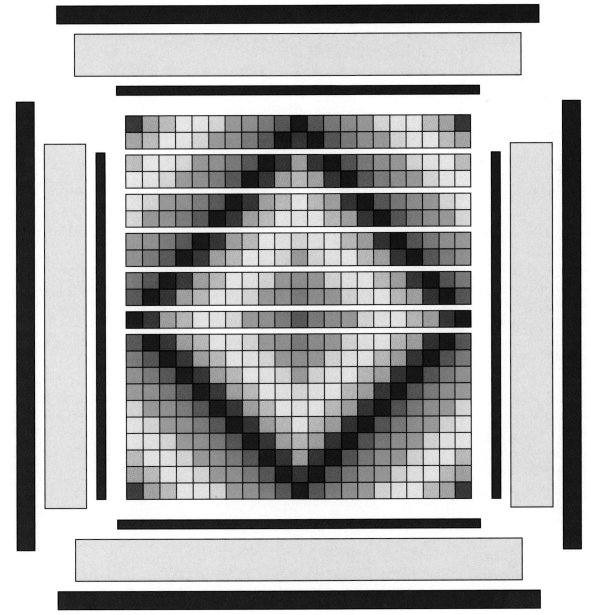

Quilt Top Assembly Diagram

Cardinals and Trees, page 44.

Quilts Made with Foundation Piecing

Most of us are immediately drawn to tiny quilts and little blocks.

But our big fingers sometimes make it hard to stitch such small quilts.

The recent revival of an old technique, paper piecing or

foundation piecing, has simplified making small blocks and complex shapes.

Getting Ready

1. Set up a lamp close to your machine. This will make it easy for you to see through the paper to the lines on the other side, so you know where to place your fabric pieces.
2. Select the fabrics you plan to use for the blocks and cut them into manageable size strips and squares.
3. Put a 90/14 needle in your sewing machine and set the stitch length to 18–20 stitches per inch. This will enable you to tear away the paper easily when you are finished.
4. Thread your needle with a neutral-colored thread.
5. Have small, sharp scissors handy.

Getting Started

1. Trace, stamp, or photocopy the design on a piece of paper. Number each section of the design to designate the sewing order. You will need a separate tracing for each block.
2. Place the fabric for piece #1 right side up on the *unmarked* side of the paper and pin. Be sure the fabric extends at least ¼" beyond all seam lines (Diagram 1).
3. Cut the approximate size of piece #2. With right sides facing, place #2 on top of #1 along the joining seam line (Diagram 2). Be sure the fabric extends at least ¼" beyond all the seam lines. Hold the paper and fabric

up to your lamp to help you see where to place the pieces.
4. Holding the fabrics in position, place the block under the presser foot with the *marked side up* and the fabrics underneath. Start the seam a few stitches before the seam line, sew the seam line between #1 and #2, and sew a few stitches beyond the end of the seam line (Diagram 3).
5. Fold the fabric open, trim, and press lightly (Diagram 4).
6. Add piece #3 across the first two pieces, stitch, open, trim, and press (Diagram 5).
7. In the same manner, add piece #4

(Diagrams 6 and 7). Continue to add pieces in numerical order until the block is complete.
8. Use an acrylic ruler and a rotary cutter to trim the block, leaving ¼" seam allowance on all sides. Remove paper.

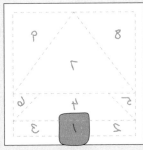

Note: All directional patterns are printed reversed since you will be stitching on the opposite side of the paper.

Diagram 1

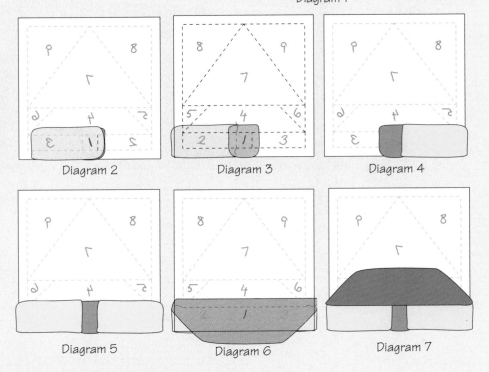

Diagram 2   Diagram 3   Diagram 4

Diagram 5   Diagram 6   Diagram 7

Cardinals and Trees

Quilt: 18" x 18"
Finished Block Size: 3½"

The cardinals in this forest of tiny trees are pieced

in two sections and then assembled.

Materials

¼ yard tan print for background
¼ yard red print I for cardinals
Scrap of black for beaks
¼ yard green print for trees
Scrap of dark red print for tree trunks
¼ yard red print II for sashing and inner border
¼ yard red-and-green plaid for outer border
⅝ yard fabric for backing
⅝ yard batting
¼ yard red print III for binding

Cutting

Tip: When sewing blocks on paper foundations, quiltmakers find that working with strips or small pieces of fabric simplifies the sewing and reduces the chance for error. The following cutting measurements are just suggestions provided for ease in handling the fabrics. See page 43 for the basics of foundation piecing.

From the *tan print,* cut:
• 1 (1¾" x 20") strip for area at tree base.
• 1 (1¼" x 10") strip for area at tree sides.
• 1 (2¼" x 30") strip for area at tree top.
• 1 (2" x 18") strip for face area of Cardinal blocks.
• 1 (3" x 18") strip for tail area of Cardinal blocks.
From *red print I,* cut:
•1 (1½" x 20") strip for breast, head, and tail.
• 1 (2½" x 18") strip. Cut strip into 4 (2½") squares for back.
From the *green print,* cut:
• 1 (1½" x 20") strip for tree base.
• 1 (3" x 20") strip for tree top.
From the *dark red print,* cut:
• 1 (1" x 5") strip for tree trunks.
From *red print II,* cut:
• 8 (1" x 18") strips. Cut 2 of the strips into 6 (1" x 4") pieces for sashing.

From the *red-and-green plaid,* cut:
• 4 (3½" x 20") strips for borders.

Assembling the Blocks

1. For Cardinal blocks, trace or photo-copy 4 of Section 1 and 4 of Section 2 onto paper. Copy 5 Tree blocks onto paper. (Patterns are on page 46.)
2. Stitch Section 1 (the head and breast) of 4 Cardinal blocks.
3. Stitch Section 2 (the back and tail) of 4 Cardinal blocks.
4. Join the 2 sections to make 4 Cardinal blocks, as shown in Cardinal Block Diagram. Trim blocks to 4" squares.
5. Stitch the Tree block in numerical order to make 5 Tree blocks, as shown in Tree Block Diagram. Trim blocks to 4" squares.

Assembling the Quilt

1. Lay out the blocks in 3 rows of 3 each, alternating them as shown in Quilt Top Assembly Diagram.
2. Sew the 6 (1" x 4") sashing pieces

between blocks in each row.
3. Sew 2 of the 1" x 18" sashing strips between the rows of blocks as shown. Sew 2 of the strips to the sides of the blocks. Sew 2 of the strips to the top and bottom of the blocks. •••••••••►

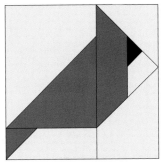
Cardinal Block Diagram

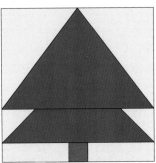
Tree Block Diagram

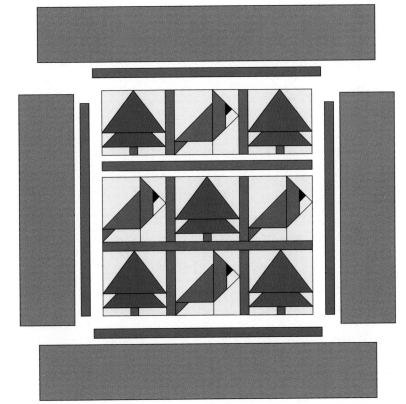
Quilt Top Assembly Diagram

Borders

1. Measure the length of the quilt top, measuring through the middle rather than along the sides. Trim 2 red-and-green plaid outer border strips to this length. Stitch 1 of these to each side of the quilt.

2. Measure the width of the quilt top, measuring through the middle rather than along the sides. Trim 2 red-and-green plaid outer border strips to this length. Stitch 1 of these to the top and bottom of the quilt.

Quilting and Finishing

1. Mark the desired quilting designs on the quilt top. The quilt shown has outline quilting around the cardinals and blocks, straight-line quilting ¼" inside the tree shapes, and straight lines in the borders.

2. Layer backing, batting, and quilt top. Baste.

3. Quilt as desired.

4. Referring to the general instructions on page 21, make 72" of bias binding and apply to quilt.

Tip: The Cardinal pattern is printed reversed since you will be stitching on the opposite side of the paper.

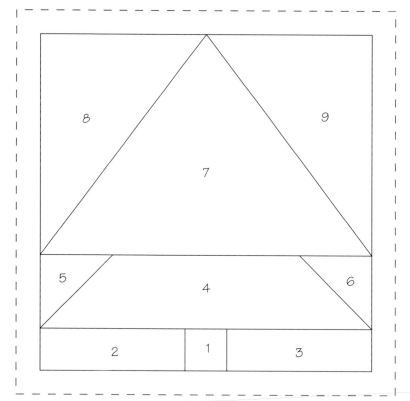

Tree Paper Piecing Pattern

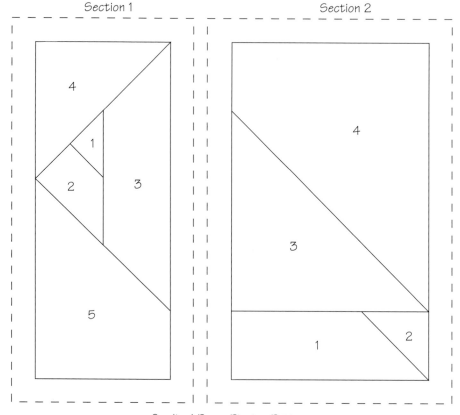

Cardinal Paper Piecing Pattern

Miniature Log Cabin

Quilt: 16" x 21"
Finished Block Size: 2½" square

Miniature Log Cabin by Mary Hickey, 1995, Keyport, Washington.

This miniature version of the quilt on page 34 uses
foundation piecing to simplify and speed its construction.

Materials

¼ yard or scrap of dark red plaid for
   center of blocks

⅛ yard or scraps of 2 dark rose prints

⅛ yard or scraps of 2 light rose prints

⅛ yard or scraps of 2 dark green prints

⅛ yard or scraps of 2 light green prints

⅛ yard or scraps of 2 dark blue prints

⅛ yard or scraps of 2 light blue prints

⅛ yard or scraps of 2 dark yellow prints

⅛ yard or scraps of 2 light yellow prints

⅛ yard light rose print for inner border

¼ yard blue floral print for outer border

½ yard fabric for backing

½ yard batting

¼ yard fabric for binding

Cutting

Tip: When sewing blocks on paper
foundations, quiltmakers find that
working with strips or small pieces of
fabric simplifies the sewing and reduces
the chance for error. The following cutting measurements are just suggestions
provided for ease in handling the fabrics. Use the same dark red for the center of all the blocks. In our sample, we
used a variety of colors in each block,
with 4 darks on 1 side of the block and
4 lights on the opposite side. See page
43 for the basics of foundation piecing.

From the *dark red plaid,* cut:
• 1 (1" x 20") strip. Cut the strip into 1"
  squares for block centers.

From each of the *light and dark prints,*
cut:
• 2 (1" x 20") strips.

From the *light rose print,* cut:
• 4 (1" x 20") strips for the inner border.

From the *blue floral print,* cut:
• 4 (2¾" x 42") strips for outer border.

Assembling the Blocks

1. Trace or photocopy 24 Miniature
Log Cabin patterns at right onto paper.

2. Pin or hold 1 dark red plaid square
(#1) on the *unmarked* side of the

paper in the center of the block.

3. Stitch 2 lights (logs #2 and #3) to
the red square in the order marked on
the paper.

4. Add 2 dark strips (logs #4 and #5)
in the same manner. Continue to add
light and dark strips until the block has
2 rows of lights and 2 rows of darks
around the central dark red square, as
shown in *Block Diagram.*

5. Make 24 blocks.

Assembling the Quilt

1. Arrange the blocks in 6 horizontal
rows of 4 blocks each as shown in the
photo.

2. Join the blocks into rows.

3. Join the rows together.

Borders

1. Measure the length of the quilt top,
measuring through the middle rather
than along the sides. Cut 2 light rose
print inner border strips to this length.
Stitch these to the sides of the quilt.

2. Measure the width of the quilt,
measuring through the middle rather
than along the ends. Cut 2 light rose
print inner border strips to this length.
Stitch these to the top and bottom of
the quilt.

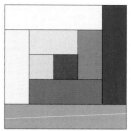

Block Diagram

3. Measure the length of the quilt top,
measuring through the middle rather
than along the sides. Cut 2 blue floral
print outer border strips to this length.
Stitch these to the sides of the quilt.

4. Measure the width of the quilt,
measuring through the middle rather
than along the ends. Trim 2 blue floral
print outer border strips to this length.
Stitch these to the top and bottom of
the quilt.

Quilting and Finishing

1. Mark the desired quilting designs
on the quilt top. The quilt shown has
diagonal quilting through the logs and
a curved design in the borders.

2. Layer backing, batting, and quilt
top. Baste.

3. Quilt as desired.

4. Referring to the general instructions
on page 21, make 74" of bias binding
and apply to quilt.

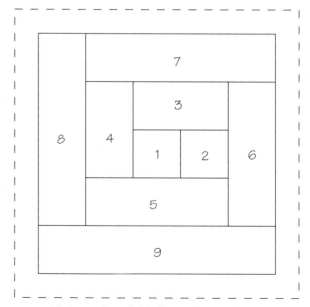

Miniature Log Cabin Paper Piecing Pattern

Flying Geese

Quilt: 14" x 16½"
Finished Geese Size: ¾" x 1½"

Flying Geese by Mary Hickey, 1995, Keyport, Washington.

I used hand-dyed fabrics in graduated shades from blue to rose to make this quilt.

But you can substitute commercially dyed fabrics for the same effect.

Materials

½ yard solid black for background, sashing, and inner and outer borders

⅛ yard each or fat eighths of 9 jewel-toned fabrics ranging from blue to purple to rose for Geese and middle border

½ yard fabric for backing

½ yard batting

¼ yard fabric for binding

Cutting

Tip: When sewing blocks on paper foundations, quiltmakers find that working with strips or small pieces of fabric simplifies the sewing and reduces the chance for error. The following cutting measurements are just suggestions provided for ease in handling the fabrics. See page 43 for the basics of foundation piecing.

From the *solid black,* cut:
• 6 (1½" x 10") strips for sashing and inner borders.
• 4 (2½" x 18") strips for outer borders.
• 6 (1½" x 18") strips for background of Geese.

From the *jewel-toned fabrics,* cut:
• 1 (2" x 18") strip of each for Geese. Cut the strips into 1¼" x 2" pieces.
• 1 (1" x 18") strip of each for inner borders.

Assembling the Blocks

1. Trace or photocopy 36 Flying Geese patterns from page 51 onto paper.
2. Referring to *Geese Block Diagram,* make 36 Flying Geese blocks. Make 4 or 5 Geese in each color.
3. Using photo as a guide, lay out blocks in 3 vertical rows of 12 geese each, turning blocks as shown. Arrange colors so that they progress from blue to purple to rose. Join blocks in each row.

Assembling the Quilt

1. Measure the length of the Flying Geese strips. (If the strips are slightly different lengths, use the measurement of the middle strip.) Cut 4 of the 6 (1½" x 10") solid black sashing and inner border strips to this length.
2. Referring to *Quilt Top Assembly Diagram,* stitch the rows together with sashing strips between them. Sew an inner border strip on each side of the Geese unit.
3. Measure the width of the quilt top, measuring through the middle rather than along the outer edges. Cut the remaining 2 solid black inner border strips to this length. Sew the strips to the top and bottom of the unit.

Borders

1. Sew 4 pairs of middle border strips end to end, grading the colors as shown in the photo.
2. Measure the length of the quilt top, measuring through the middle rather than along the sides. Trim 2 pair of middle border strips to this length. Stitch 1 of these to each side of the quilt.
3. Measure the width of the quilt top, measuring through the middle rather than along the sides. Trim 2 pairs of middle border strips to this length. Stitch 1 of these to the top and bottom of the quilt.
4. Measure the length of the quilt top, measuring through the middle rather than along the sides. Trim 2 black outer border strips to this length. Stitch these to the sides of the quilt.

Geese Block Diagram

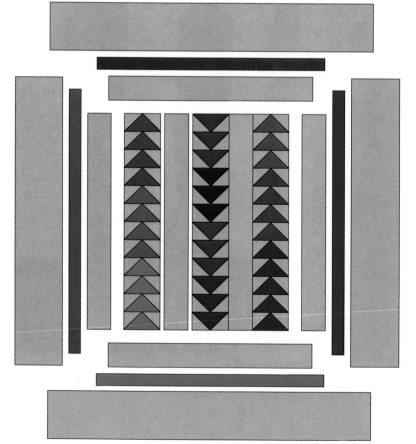

Quilt Top Assembly Diagram

5. Measure the width of the quilt top, measuring through the middle rather than along the sides. Trim 2 black outer border strips to this length. Stitch these to the top and bottom of the quilt.

Quilting and Finishing

1. Mark the desired quilting designs on the quilt top. The quilt shown has outline quilting around the Geese strips and inner borders and a curved design in the outer borders.

2. Layer backing, batting, and quilt top. Baste.

3. Quilt as desired.

4. Referring to the general instructions on page 21, make 61" of bias binding and apply to the quilt.

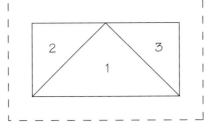
Flying Geese Paper Piecing Pattern

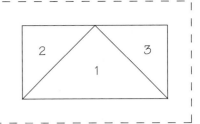
Flying Geese Paper Piecing Pattern

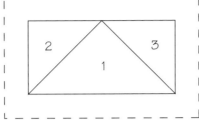
Flying Geese Paper Piecing Pattern

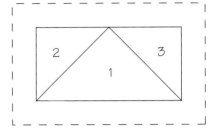
Flying Geese Paper Piecing Pattern

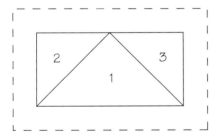
Flying Geese Paper Piecing Pattern

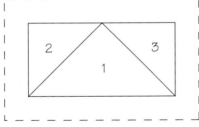
Flying Geese Paper Piecing Pattern

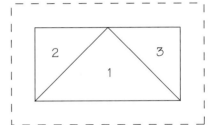
Flying Geese Paper Piecing Pattern

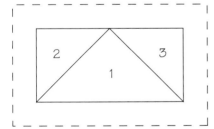
Flying Geese Paper Piecing Pattern

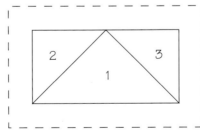
Flying Geese Paper Piecing Pattern

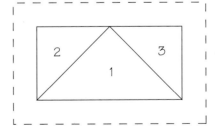
Flying Geese Paper Piecing Pattern

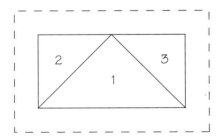
Flying Geese Paper Piecing Pattern

Tip: Since you need so many paper patterns for this quilt, here are some extras so that you can make fewer photocopies.

Flying Geese 51

Ozark Tiles

Quilt: 14" x 16"
Finished Block Size: 2" square

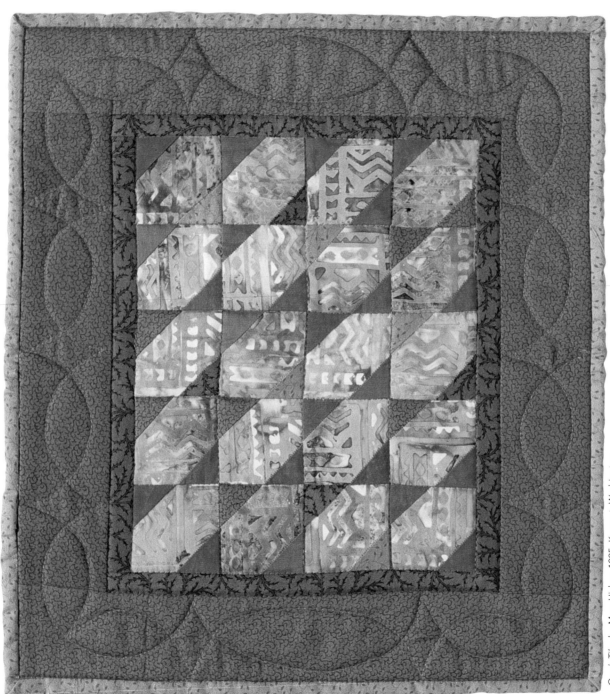

Ozark Tiles by Mary Hickey, 1995, Keyport, Washington.

This humble block, two triangles sewn to opposite corners of a square,

becomes a small work of art when pieced with carefully chosen fabrics.

Materials

¼ yard multicolored print for background

¼ yard teal print for corners and outer border

⅛ yard rose print for corners and inner border

½ yard fabric for backing

½ yard batting

¼ yard fabric for binding

Cutting

Tip: When sewing blocks on paper foundations, quiltmakers find that working with strips or small pieces of fabric simplifies the sewing and reduces the chance for error. The following cutting measurements are just suggestions provided for ease in handling the fabrics. See page 43 for the basics of foundation piecing.

From *multicolored print,* cut:
• 20 (2½") squares.

From the *teal print,* cut:
• 36 (1½") squares for corners.
• 4 (2¾" x 18") strips for outer borders.

From the *rose print,* cut:
• 4 (1½") squares for corners.
• 4 (1" x 18") strips for inner borders.

Assembling the Blocks

1. Trace or photocopy 20 Ozark Tile patterns at right onto paper.

2. Pin or hold a print square (#1) on the *unmarked* side of the paper in the center of the block.

3. Stitch 1 teal square to each corner (#2 and #3) as marked on the paper.

4. Repeat to make 20 blocks, as shown in *Block Diagram,* adding 1 rose corner to 4 of the blocks.

Tip: For added visual interest, use a variety of teal prints in the corners.

Assembling the Quilt

1. Arrange blocks into 5 horizontal rows of 4 blocks each as shown in the photo.

2. Join the blocks into rows.

3. Join the rows together.

Borders

1. Measure the length of the quilt top, measuring through the middle rather than along the sides. Cut 2 rose print inner border strips to this length. Stitch these to the sides of the quilt.

2. Measure the width of the quilt, measuring through the middle rather than along the ends. Cut 2 rose print inner border strips to this length. Stitch these to the top and bottom of the quilt.

3. Measure the length of the quilt top, measuring through the middle rather than along the sides. Cut 2 teal print outer border strips to this length. Stitch these to the sides of the quilt.

4. Measure the width of the quilt, measuring through the middle rather than along the ends. Trim 2 teal print outer border strips to this length. Stitch these to the top and bottom of the quilt.

Quilting and Finishing

1. Mark the desired quilting designs on the quilt top. The quilt shown has in-the-ditch quilting around the blocks and a curved design in the outer border.

2. Layer backing, batting, and quilt top. Baste.

3. Quilt as desired.

4. Referring to the general instructions on page 21, make 70" of bias binding and apply to the quilt.

Block Diagram

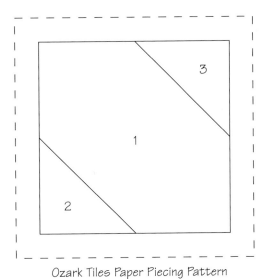

Tip: This pattern is printed reversed since you will be stitching on the opposite side of the paper.

Ozark Tiles Paper Piecing Pattern

Keyport Shores, page 74.

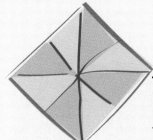

Quilts Made with Half-Square Triangles

Clever quiltmakers have developed many smart methods for piecing the shapes

that make up block designs. Speed piecing is a combination of rotary cutting and efficient sewing techniques.

Try this method of making squares from half-square triangles. The instructions for each

quilt will tell you what size the initial fabric piece should be and how wide to cut

your strips. You will need a ruler with a 45° diagonal line.

Once you have practiced this method, you will find that it is the fastest and most accurate way to make half-square triangles. Plus, you will have done all the sewing and pressing before you cut the squares.

Half-square Triangles

1. Cut a piece of two different fabrics. (The size you need for each quilt will be specified in the instructions.)

2. Layer both fabrics with right sides facing up (Diagram 1).

3. With the fabrics layered, place your ruler from corner to corner and make a diagonal cut (Diagram 2).

4. Cut strips parallel to the diagonal cut (Diagram 3). The strips must be ½" wider than the finished square. Each set of quilt instructions will tell you how wide to cut the bias strips.

5. Rearrange the strips to make two square strip sets, alternating the colors (Diagram 4). The corner pieces in each unit will be different colors.

6. Sew the strips in each strip set together, offsetting the tops ¼" as shown in Diagram 5. Press all seams toward the darker color. The resulting unit should resemble Diagram 6.

7. Position your ruler with the 45°-angle line on the middle seam and trim the edge as shown. (Diagram 7).

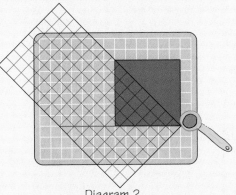

Diagram 1   Diagram 2

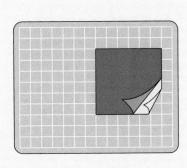

Diagram 3   Diagram 4

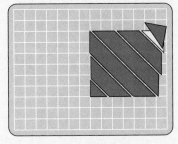

Offset each end ¼".

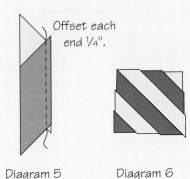

Diagram 5   Diagram 6

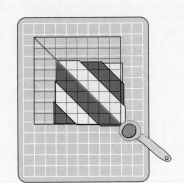

Diagram 7

8. Cut a segment from the strip set as shown in *Diagram 8*. The segment must be ½" wider than the finished square. Each set of quilt instructions will tell you how wide to cut the segment. Continue cutting in this manner, trimming edges evenly as needed (*Diagram 9*).

9. Working with one cut segment, place a square ruler so that the edge of the ruler is on the cut edge of the fabric and the diagonal line is on the seam line as shown. Cut on the right side of the ruler (*Diagram 10*).

10. Position the ruler on each seam line in this segment in the same manner and trim, creating rectangles (*Diagram 11*).

11. Turn the cut pieces around so that the untrimmed edge is on the right. Reposition the ruler so that the edge of the ruler is on the edge of the fabric and the diagonal line is on the seam and cut, creating pieced squares (*Diagram 12*).

12. Before you cut another segment from the strip set, be sure to place the ruler so that the diagonal line is on the seam line and trim the edge.

13. Check to be sure that the pieced square is exactly ½" larger than the finished size.

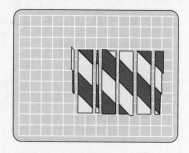
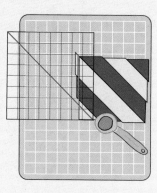

Diagram 8

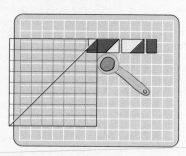

Diagram 9

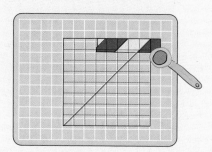

Diagram 10

Diagram 11

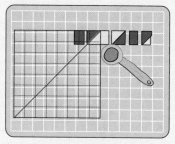

Diagram 12

Maple Leaves

Quilt: 31½" x 39½"
Finished Block Size: 6" square

A collection of pastel scraps finds a home in these lovely leaves. Arranging the blocks with the

lighter leaves on top and the darker ones near the bottom balances the design.

A wide border of decorator chintz unifies all the colors in the blocks.

Materials

½ yard muslin for background

¼ yard or scraps of 13 different fabrics for leaves

¼ yard peach print for sashing

¼ yard green print for inner border

½ yard multicolor print for outer border

1⅛ yards fabric for backing

1⅛ yards batting

⅜ yard green print for binding

Cutting

From the *muslin,* cut:

• 2 (6"-wide) strips. Cut strips into 13 (6") squares.

• 1 (2½"-wide) strip. Cut strip into 13 (2½") squares.

From each of the *¼ yard or scraps of 13 different fabrics,* cut:

• 1 (6") square.

• 1 (2½") square.

• 1 (2½" x 4½") rectangle.

• 1 (1" x 4½") strip.

From the *peach print,* cut:

• 8 (2½" x 6½") pieces.

• 4 (4½" x 6½") pieces.

From the *green print,* cut:

• 4 (1¾" x 42") strips.

From the *multicolor print,* cut:

• 4 (4¼" x 42") strips.

Assembling the Blocks

1. Referring to the general instructions for making squares from half-square triangles on pages 55–56, use the 6" squares each of muslin and scraps for leaves to make 4 (2½") half-square triangle units of each color as follows:

• Cut the bias strips 2½".

• Cut the segments 2½".

• Cut the squares 2½".

2. To make the stem, fold each of the 1" x 4½" leaf fabric strips in half lengthwise with wrong sides facing and press (Diagram 1).

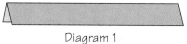

Diagram 1

3. Fold 1 (2½") muslin square in half diagonally and press a crease, as shown in Diagram 2. Then unfold the square.

4. Place 1 folded strip to the right of the crease on 1 muslin square, with the raw edges of the strip exactly on the crease. Stitch the strip to the muslin ⅛" from the raw edge (Diagram 3).

5. Fold the sewn strip over to the left and hand- or machine-stitch along the left edge (Diagram 4). Repeat steps 3–5 for each stem.

6. Arrange the pieces for each block as shown in the Block Assembly Diagram. Join the pieces into 3 vertical rows; then join rows as shown in the Block Diagram. Repeat to make 13 blocks.

Assembling the Quilt

1. For Row 1, join 3 blocks in a row with 2 (2½" x 6½") sashing pieces between the blocks, as shown in the Quilt Top Assembly Diagram. Make Row 3 and 5 in the same manner, turning blocks as shown.

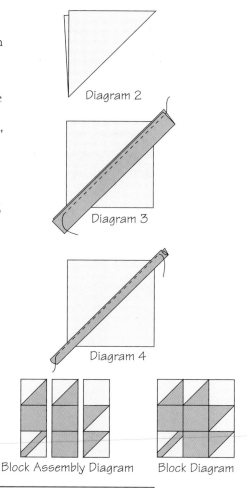

Diagram 2

Diagram 3

Diagram 4

Block Assembly Diagram   Block Diagram

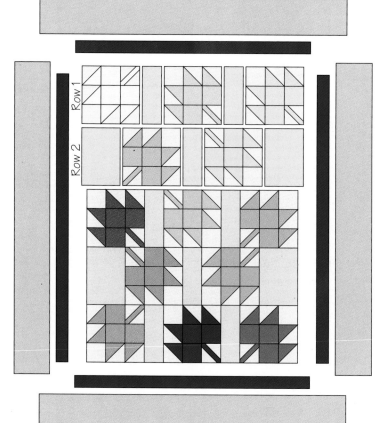

Quilt Top Assembly Diagram

2. For Row 2, join 2 blocks in a row with 1 (2½" x 6½") sashing piece between the blocks and 1 (4½" x 6½") sashing piece on each end, as shown in the *Quilt Top Assembly Diagram*. Make Row 4 in the same manner, turning blocks as shown.

3. Alternating the rows as shown, join the rows to create the quilt top.

Borders

1. Measure the length of the quilt top, measuring through the middle rather than along the sides. Trim 2 green print inner border strips to this length. Stitch 1 of these to each side of the quilt.

2. Measure the width of the quilt top, measuring through the middle rather than along the sides. Trim 2 green print inner border strips to this length. Stitch to the top and bottom of the quilt.

3. Measure the length of the quilt top, measuring through the middle rather than along the sides. Trim 2 multi-color print outer border strips to this length. Stitch 1 of these to each side of the quilt.

4. Measure the width of the quilt top, measuring through the middle rather than along the sides. Trim 2 multi-color print outer border strips to this length. Stitch 1 of these to the top and bottom of the quilt.

Quilting and Finishing

1. Mark the desired quilting designs on the quilt top. The quilt shown has outline quilting around the shapes in the leaf blocks, an oak leaf in the sashing pieces, straight-line quilting in the inner border, and a leaf pattern in the outer border.

2. Layer backing, batting, and quilt top. Baste.

3. Quilt as desired.

4. Referring to the general instructions on page 21, make 140" of bias binding and apply to the quilt.

A Quick Reference for Fraction-to-Decimal Equivalents

Often it is helpful to know fraction-to-decimal equivalents so that you can quickly do quilt math on your calculator. This can be especially helpful when estimating your fabric cost. For example, if you have your eye on a fabric that costs $8.40 a yard and you need 1¾ yards for your quilt, multiply $8.40 by 1.75 to get a cost of $14.70.

Inches	Fractions	Decimals
⅛"		.125"
¼"		.25"
⅜"		.375"
½"		.5"
¾"		.75"
1"		1.0"
4½"	⅛ yard	.125 yard
9"	¼ yard	.25 yard
12"	⅓ yard	.333 yard
13½"	⅜ yard	.375 yard
18"	½ yard	.5 yard
22½"	⅝ yard	.625 yard
27"	¾ yard	.75 yard
31½"	⅞ yard	.875 yard
36"	1 yard	1.0 yard

See page 80 for a chart on how to convert inches and yards to centimeters and meters.

Weather Vane

Quilt: 29¾" x 40¼"
Finished Block Size: 8¾" square

Weather Vane by Helen Hickey, 1995, Camp Grove, Illinois.

While it may not tell you which way the wind is blowing, this quilt will tell you

that the rich colors of autumn are on the way.

Pick a pack of warm colors and make your own special Weather Vane.

Materials

⅞ yard beige print for background
¼ yard dark rust print for squares
⅝ yard medium rust print for triangles
¼ yard light peach print for squares
⅛ yard dark green print for squares
½ yard light green print for sashing
   and inner border
½ yard scalloped rust print fabric for
   border
1 yard fabric for backing
1¼ yards batting
⅜ yard fabric for binding

Cutting

From the *beige print,* cut:
• 1 (18" x 21") piece.
• 5 (2¼" x 42") strips. Cut 2 of the
   strips into 24 (2¼") squares for the
   outer corners of the blocks.
From the *dark rust print,* cut:
• 2 (2¼" x 42") strips.
From the *medium rust print,* cut:
• 1 (18" x 21") piece.
From the *light peach print,* cut:
• 3 (2¼" x 42") strips. Cut 1 strip into
   12 (2¼") squares for the top and
   bottom of the blocks.
From the *dark green print,* cut:
• 1 (2¼" x 42") strip.
From the *light green print,* cut:
• 7 (2¼" x 42") strips.
From the *scalloped rust print,* cut:
• 4 (3¾" x 42") strips.

Assembling the Blocks

1. Referring to the general instructions
for making squares from half-square
triangles on pages 55–56, use the 18" x
21" pieces each of beige and medium
rust to make 48 (2¼") half-square triangle units as follows:
• Cut the bias strips 2¼".
• Cut the segments 2¼".
• Cut the squares 2¼".
2. Stitch 1 (42"-long) beige strip to 1
(42"-long) peach strip to make a strip
set (Diagram 1). Make 2 strip sets.
3. Join strip sets made in Step 2 to

each side of 1 dark green strip as
shown in Diagram 2. Cut the strip set
into 6 (2¼") segments.
4. Join strips to make dark rust/beige/
dark rust strip set. Cut the strip set into
12 (2¼") segments (Diagram 3).
5. Referring to *Block Assembly Diagram,* arrange the pieces as shown.
6. Join the pieces as shown in the *Block
Diagram* to make 6 blocks.

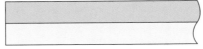

Diagram 1

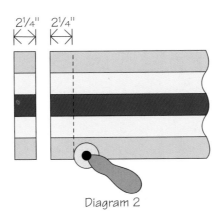

Diagram 2

Diagram 3

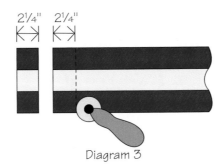

Block Assembly Diagram

Assembling the Quilt

From 5 of the light green print sashing
strips, cut:
• 3 (2¼" x 9¼") pieces. Sew 1 of these
between each block pair.
• 2 (2¼" x 19¾") pieces. Sew 1 of these
between block rows.
• 2 (2¼" x 29¾") pieces. Sew these to
the sides of the quilt.
• 2 (2¼" x 22¾") pieces. Sew these to
the top and bottom of the quilt.

Borders

1. Measure the length of the quilt top,
measuring through the middle rather
than along the sides. Trim 2 scalloped
rust print outer border strips to this
length. Stitch 1 of these to each side of
the quilt.
2. Measure the width of the quilt top,
measuring through the middle rather
than along the sides. Trim 2 scalloped
rust print outer border strips to this
length. Stitch 1 of these to the top and
bottom of the quilt.

Quilting and Finishing

1. Mark the desired quilting designs
on the quilt top. The quilt shown has
outline quilting around the Weather
Vane blocks and sashing strips, and
straight-line quilting in the borders.
2. Layer backing, batting, and quilt
top. Baste.
3. Quilt as desired.
4. Referring to the general instructions
on page 21, make 140" of bias binding
and apply to the quilt.

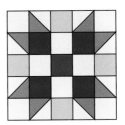

Block Diagram

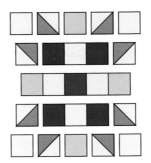

Churn Dash

Quilt: 35" x 40"
Finished Block Size: 5" square

Churn Dash by Mary Hickey, 1994, Keyport, Washington.

Scraps of warm reds, moss greens, and rich navies recreate the atmosphere of

an old farmhouse in this Churn Dash. Most of the blocks use the darks on

beige or light tan backgrounds. However, three of the blocks took on a life of their own

by reversing the color placement. Can you find them?

Materials

1¼ yards tan print for background
1¼ yards navy print for triangles,
   squares, and border
¾ yard red print for triangles and
   squares
¼ yard green print for triangles and
   squares
½ yard plaid for sashing
1¼ yards fabric for backing
1¼ yards batting
⅜ yard fabric for binding

Cutting

From the *tan print,* cut:
• 2 (18" x 20") pieces.
• 1 (9") square.
• 4 (1½" x 42") strips. Cut the strips
   into 97 (1½") squares.
From the *navy print,* cut:
• 1 (18" x 20") piece.
• 2 (1½" x 42") strips. Cut the strips
   into 36 (1½") squares.
• 4 (5½" x 42") strips for borders.
From the *red print,* cut:
• 1 (18" x 20") piece.
• 3 (1½" x 42") strips. Cut the strips
   into 37 (1½") squares for blocks.
From the *green print,* cut:
• 1 (9") square.
• 1 (1½" x 20") strip. Cut the strip into
   10 (1½") squares.
From the *plaid,* cut:
• 7 (1½" x 42") strips. Cut the strips
   into 49 (1½" x 5½") strips.

Assembling the Blocks

1. Referring to the general instructions
for making squares from half-square
triangles on pages 55–56, use the 18" x
20" pieces of tan and navy, the 18" x
20" pieces of tan and red, and the 9"
squares of tan and green to make 2½"
half-square triangle units as follows:
• Cut the bias strips 2½".
• Cut the segments 2½".
• Cut the squares 2½".
Make 44 tan and navy half-square
triangle units.

Make 32 tan and red half-square
triangle units.
Make 4 tan and green half-square
triangle units.
2. Referring to *Block Assembly Diagram,*
arrange the pieces as shown. Join units
into 3 vertical rows; then join rows.
3. Make 11 blocks with navy triangles
(Block Diagram), 8 blocks with red triangles, and 1 block with green triangles. (Feel free to vary the triangles and
the colors of the small squares in each
block. Notice that in our sample, 3 of
the blocks have the tan and colors in
reverse positions.)

Assembling the Quilt

1. Join 4 plaid sashing pieces with 5
red squares as shown in *Diagram* 1.
Make 6 sashing rows.
2. Join 4 blocks in a horizontal row
with a sashing strip between each block
and on each end of the row. Make 5
block rows as shown in *Diagram* 2.
3. Referring to *Quilt Top Assembly
Diagram,* join the block rows with the
sashing rows.
4. Join a sashing row to the top and

bottom of the quilt, as shown in *Quilt
Top Assembly Diagram.*

Borders

1. Measure the length of the quilt top,
measuring through the middle rather
than along the sides. Trim 2 navy print
outer border strips to this length. Stitch
1 of these to each side of the quilt.
2. Measure the width of the quilt top,
measuring through the middle rather
than along the sides. Trim 2 navy print
outer border strips to this length. Stitch
to the top and bottom of the quilt.

Quilting and Finishing

1. Mark the desired quilting designs
on the quilt top. The quilt shown has
outline quilting around the shapes in
the Churn Dash blocks, a double line
in each sashing piece and red square,
and a cable design in the border.
2. Layer backing, batting, and quilt
top. Baste.
3. Quilt as desired.
4. Referring to the general instructions
on page 21, make 150" of bias binding
and apply to the quilt.

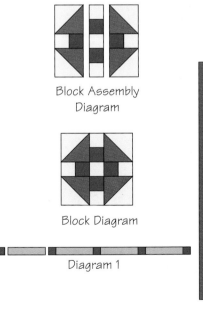

Block Assembly
Diagram

Block Diagram

Diagram 1

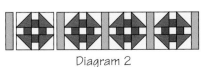

Diagram 2

Quilt Top Assembly Diagram

 Churn Dash   63

Contrary Wife

Quilt: 36" x 36"
Finished Block Size: 6" square

Contrary Wife by Mary Hickey, 1994, Keyport, Washington. Quilted by the Ohio Amish.

Contrary Wife blocks made in four colorways give the illusion of diagonal lines

skimming across the quilt, providing a sense of movement.

Variable stars also appear in the lighter center.

Materials

¾ yard light peach print for triangles and squares

½ yard dark peach print for squares

¾ yard dark rust print for triangles and squares

¾ yard light blue print for triangles

½ yard medium blue print for squares

¾ yard dark blue print for triangles

1⅛ yards fabric for backing

1⅛ yards batting

¼ yard fabric for binding

Cutting

From the *light peach print,* cut:
• 3 (9" x 20") pieces.
• 2 (2½" x 42") strips. Cut strips into 24 (2½") squares.

From the *dark peach print,* cut:
• 5 (2½" x 42") strips. Cut strips into 66 (2½") squares.

From the *rust print,* cut:
• 3 (9" x 20") pieces.

From the *light blue print,* cut:
• 3 (9" x 20") pieces.
• 2 (2½" x 40") strips. Cut strips into 24 (2½") squares.

From the *medium blue print,* cut:
• 5 (2½" x 42") strips. Cut strips into 66 (2½") squares.

From the *dark blue print,* cut:
• 3 (9" x 20") pieces.

Assembling the Blocks

1. Referring to the general instructions for making squares from half-square triangles on pages 55–56, use the 3 (9" x 20") pieces each of light peach and rust to make 72 (2½") half-square triangle units as follows:
• Cut the bias strips 2½".
• Cut the segments 2½".
• Cut the squares 2½".

2. Referring to the general instructions for making squares from half-square triangles on pages 55–56, use the 3 (9" x 20") pieces each of light blue and dark blue to make 72 (2½") half-square triangle units as follows:
• Cut the bias strips 2½".
• Cut the segments 2½".
• Cut the squares 2½".

3. Referring to *Block Diagrams,* arrange the pieces in the order in which they appear in the blocks. Make the number of blocks indicated.

Assembling the Quilt

1. Join the blocks into 6 rows of 6 blocks each, alternating blocks as shown in *Quilt Top Assembly Diagram.*

2. Join the rows together to create the quilt top.

Quilting and Finishing

1. Mark the desired quilting designs on the quilt top. The quilt shown has a diagonal line quilted through all the squares, creating a diagonal grid over the entire quilt.

2. Layer backing, batting, and quilt top. Baste.

3. Quilt as desired.

4. Referring to the general instructions on page 21, make 152" of bias binding and apply to the quilt.

Block 1 Diagram
Make 8.

Block 2 Diagram
Make 10.

Block 3 Diagram
Make 8.

Block 4 Diagram
Make 10.

Quilt Top Assembly Diagram

Birds in the Air

Quilt: 33" x 45"
Finished Block Size: 6" square

Birds in the Air by Mary Hickey, 1995, Keyport, Washington.

A birdhouse fabric adds a touch of humor to these cheerful Birds in the Air blocks. Since each block has a diagonal seam across its center, you can rearrange them in several ways to create various designs.

Materials

⅜ yard light blue print for large and small triangles

⅜ yard dark blue print for small triangles

⅜ yard light red print for large and small triangles

⅜ yard dark red print for small triangles

⅜ yard light purple print for large and small triangles

⅜ yard dark purple print for small triangles

⅜ yard light yellow print for large and small triangles

⅜ yard dark yellow print for small triangles

½ yard light green print for large and small triangles and inner border

¾ yard dark green print for small triangles and outer border

¼ yard novelty print for large triangles

1¼ yards backing fabric

1¼ yards batting

¾ yard fabric for binding

Cutting

From the *light blue print*, cut:
• 1 (9" x 20") piece.
• 3 (6⅞") squares. Cut the squares in half diagonally.

From the *dark blue print*, cut:
• 1 (9" x 20") piece.
• 9 (2⅞") squares. Cut the squares in half diagonally.

From the *light red print*, cut:
• 1 (9" x 20") piece.
• 2 (6⅞") squares. Cut the squares in half diagonally.

From the *dark red print*, cut:
• 1 (9" x 20") piece.
• 6 (2⅞") squares. Cut the squares in half diagonally.

From the *light purple print*, cut:
• 1 (9" x 20") piece.
• 2 (6⅞") squares. Cut the squares in half diagonally.

From the *dark purple print*, cut:
• 1 (9" x 20") piece.
• 6 (2⅞") squares. Cut the squares in half diagonally.

From the *light yellow print*, cut:
• 1 (9" x 20") piece.
• 2 (6⅞") squares. Cut the squares in half diagonally.

From the *dark yellow print*, cut:
• 1 (9" x 20") piece.
• 5 (2⅞") squares. Cut the squares in half diagonally.

From the *light green print*, cut:
• 1 (9" x 20") piece.
• 1 (6⅞") square. Cut the square in half diagonally.
• 4 (2" x 42") strips.

From the *dark green print*, cut:
• 1 (9" x 20") piece.
• 11 (2⅞") squares. Cut the squares in half diagonally.
• 4 (3¼" x 42") strips.

From the *novelty print*, cut:
• 3 (6⅞") squares. Cut the squares in half diagonally.

Assembling the Blocks

1. Referring to the general instructions for making squares from half-square triangles on pages 55–56, use the light and dark 9" x 20" pieces of each color to make 3 half-square triangle units for each block as follows:
• Cut the bias strips 2½".
• Cut the segments 2½".
• Cut the squares 2½".

2. Referring to Block Assembly Diagram, arrange the pieces for each block as shown. Join the triangle-squares and small triangles in vertical rows and then join rows to make a large pieced triangle. Join the pieced triangle to a matching light triangle to complete the block (Block Diagram).

3. Make 6 blue blocks, 4 red blocks, 4 purple blocks, 3 yellow blocks, 6 green blocks with the novelty fabric in the large triangles, and 1 green block with the light green fabric in the large triangle.

Block Assembly Diagram  Block Diagram

Quilt Top Assembly Diagram

Assembling the Quilt

1. Arrange the blocks in 6 horizontal rows of 4 blocks each as shown in the Quilt Top Assembly Diagram (page 67).
2. Join the blocks in each row.
3. Join the rows to form the quilt top.

Borders

1. Measure the length of the quilt top, measuring through the middle rather than along the sides. Trim 2 light green border strips to this length. Stitch 1 of these to each side of the quilt.
2. Measure the width of the quilt top, measuring through the middle rather than along the sides. Trim 2 light green border strips to this length. Stitch to the top and bottom of the quilt.
3. Measure the length of the quilt top, measuring through the middle rather than along the sides. Trim 2 dark green border strips to this length. Stitch 1 of these to each side of the quilt.
4. Measure the width of the quilt top, measuring through the middle rather than along the sides. Trim 2 dark green border strips to this length. Stitch 1 of these to the top and bottom of the quilt.

Quilting and Finishing

1. Mark the desired quilting designs on the quilt top. The quilt shown has outline quilting in the small triangles, a portion of a sunflower in the large triangles, a simple cable design in the inner border, and a Celtic cable in the outer border.
2. Layer backing, batting, and quilt top. Baste.
3. Quilt as desired.
4. Referring to the general instructions on page 21, make 156" of bias binding and apply to the quilt.

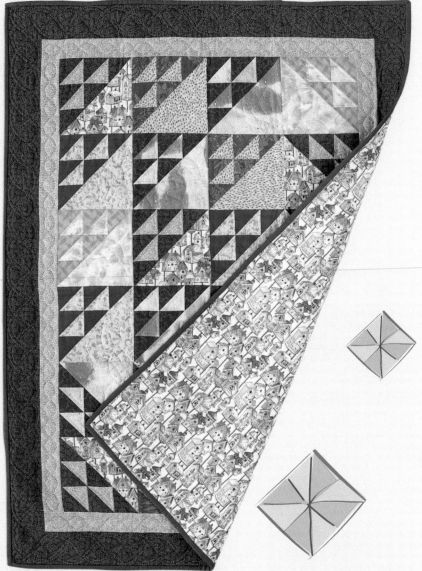

Use a Complementary Fabric for Your Backing

This whimsical birdhouse print backing complements the Birds in the Air blocks on the front. For continuity, use the backing fabric in a few of the quilt blocks.

Pinwheels

Quilt: 33" x 33"
Finished Block Size: 3" square

This small quilt, inspired by a masterpiece sewn during the War of 1812, uses simple indigo pinwheels combined with triangle setting blocks. Look for five shades of one color to create dimension within the setting blocks.

Materials

1½ yards white print for background

⅜ yard each of 4 different navy blue prints

¼ yard light blue print for inner set blocks

¼ yard medium blue print for middle set blocks

¼ yard blue print for outer set blocks

½ yard dark blue print for border

1 yard fabric for backing

1 yard batting

⅝ yard fabric for binding

Cutting

From the *white print*, cut:

• 4 (9" x 20") pieces.

• 1 (18" x 20") piece.

• 1 (3½") square for center block.

• 3 (10") squares.

• 4 (5¼") squares.

• 4 (3⅞") squares. Cut the squares in half diagonally for the corner set pieces.

From the *navy blue prints*, cut:

• 1 (9" x 20") piece from each.

From the *light blue print*, cut:

• 2 (10") squares.

From the *medium blue print*, cut:

• 1 (18" x 20") piece.

• 1 (10") square.

From the *blue print*, cut:

• 5 (5¼") squares. Cut the squares in quarters diagonally for the side triangles.

• 2 (3½") squares. Cut the squares in half diagonally for the corner triangles.

From the *dark blue print*, cut:

• 4 (4" x 42") strips.

Assembling the Blocks

1. Referring to the general instructions for making squares from half-square triangles on pages 55–56, use the 9" x 20" pieces of white and navy to make 144 (2") half-square triangle units as follows:

• Cut the bias strips 2¼".

• Cut the segments 2".

• Cut the squares 2".

2. Arrange 4 units as shown in the Block Assembly Diagram. Join the units in pairs; then join pairs as shown in the Block Diagram. Repeat to form 36 Pinwheel blocks.

3. Referring to the general instructions for making half-square triangles on pages 55–56, use the 18" x 20" pieces of white and medium blue for middle set blocks to make 12 (3½") half-square triangle blocks (Diagram 1) as follows:

• Cut the bias strips 3½".

• Cut the segments 3½".

• Cut the squares 3½".

4. Referring to the general instructions for making quarter-square triangles on pages 87–88, use 1 (10") square each of white and medium blue for middle set blocks to make 4 (3½") quarter-square triangle blocks as follows:

• Cut the bias strips 4".

• Cut the segments 4".

• Cut the squares 4".

Cut the squares in half diagonally. Join 1 half with 1 white triangle, as shown in Diagram 2. Make 4 units.

5. Referring to the general instructions for making half-square triangles on pages 55–56, use 1 (10") square of white and light blue for inner set blocks to make 4 (3½") half-square triangle blocks as follows:

• Cut the bias strips 3½".

• Cut the segments 3½".

• Cut the squares 3½".

6. Referring to the general instructions for making quarter-square triangles on pages 87–88, use the 10" squares of white and light blue for inner set blocks to make 2 (3½") quarter-square triangle blocks as follows:

• Cut the bias strips 4".

• Cut the segments 4".

• Cut the squares 4".

Cut the squares in half diagonally. Join 1 half with 1 white triangle. Make 4 units.

Block Assembly Diagram   Block Diagram

Diagram 1   Diagram 2

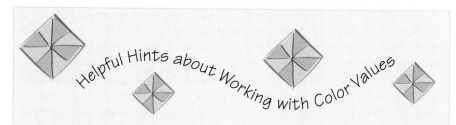

Helpful Hints about Working with Color Values

When a materials list calls for several different values of the same color, as in *Pinwheels,* it may be helpful to use a tool called a Ruby Beholder™. This is a thick, plastic bar (usually red) that, when held against fabrics, lets you quickly see what reads as a light, medium, or dark. If you do not have this tool, a colored transparent sheet, like those used in school notebooks, also works.

Assembling the Quilt

1. Arrange the blocks and set pieces as shown in the *Quilt Top Assembly Diagram*.

2. Join the pieces in diagonal rows.

3. Join the rows together to form the quilt top.

Borders

1. Measure the length of the quilt top, measuring through the middle rather than along the sides. Trim 2 dark blue print border strips to this length. Stitch 1 of these to each side of the quilt.

2. Measure the width of the quilt top, measuring through the middle rather than along the sides. Trim 2 dark blue print border strips to this length. Stitch 1 to the top and bottom of the quilt.

Quilting and Finishing

1. Mark the desired quilting designs on the quilt top. The quilt shown has outline quilting in the Pinwheel blocks, a four-leaf design in the set blocks, and a curly wave design in the border.

2. Layer backing, batting, and quilt top. Baste.

3. Quilt as desired.

4. Referring to the general instructions on page 21, make 132" of bias binding and apply to the quilt.

Quilt Top Assembly Diagram

Bear's Paw

Quilt: 39½" x 39½"
Finished Block Size: 10½" square

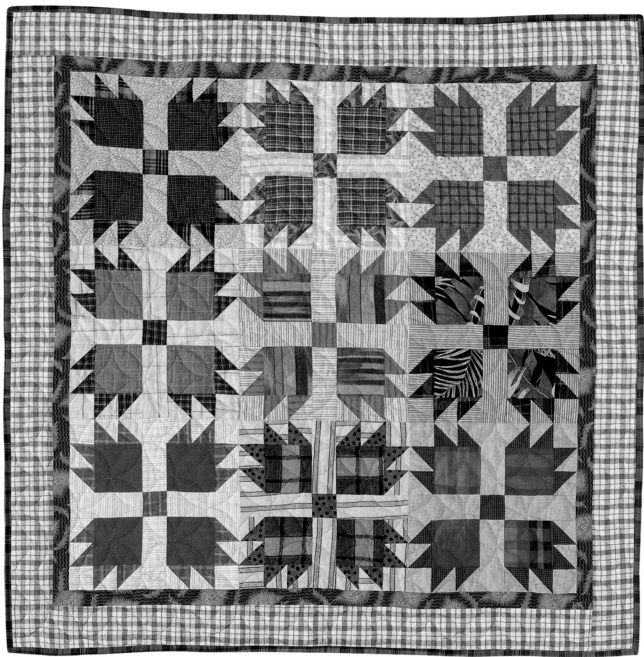

Bear's Paw by Terri Shinn, 1995, Snohomish, Washington.

Bold and masculine, these Bear's Paw blocks make you long to hibernate.

Don't fuss over matching the plaids or worry too much about their grain lines.

A carefree hand in using plaids adds to the charm of the piece.

Materials

1¼ yards of neutral scraps in plaids, stripes, and small prints for backgrounds

1¾ yards of dark scraps in red, brown, green, and orange prints for the Bear's Paw (quilt shown uses 18 different fabrics)

¼ yard rust print for inner border

½ yard tan-and-red plaid for outer border

1¼ yards fabric for backing

1¼ yards batting

⅜ yard fabric for binding

Cutting

From the *neutral background prints*, cut:
- 9 (9") squares.
- 5 (2" x 42") strips. Cut strips into 36 (2" x 5") pieces.
- 36 (2") squares.

From each of *9 different dark scraps*, cut:
- 1 (9") square for toes.
- 1 (2") square for center square.

From each of *remaining 9 dark scraps*, cut:
- 1 (3½" x 20") strips. Cut strip into 4 (3½") squares for paws.

From the *rust print*, cut:
- 4 (1½" x 42") strips.

From the *tan-and-red plaid*, cut:
- 4 (3½" x 42") strips.

Assembling the Blocks

1. Referring to the general instructions for making squares from half-square triangles on pages 55–56, use the 9" squares of neutral and dark scraps to make 144 (2") half-square triangle units, 16 from each fabric combination as follows:
- Cut the bias strips 2¼".
- Cut the segments 2".
- Cut the squares 2".

2. Join 16 matching half-square triangle units (bear toes) together in pairs. Be careful to join the background color to the darker color as shown in Diagram 1.

3. Arrange the matching pieces for each paw unit as shown in Diagram 2. Make 4 units for each block.

4. Arrange the pieces for each block as shown in the Block Assembly Diagram. Join the pieces into vertical rows; then join rows to complete the block. Make 9 blocks.

Assembling the Quilt

1. Join the blocks in 3 horizontal rows of 3 blocks each as shown in Quilt Top Assembly Diagram. Pin and carefully sew all match points.

2. Join the rows together to complete the quilt top.

Borders

1. Measure the length of the quilt top, measuring through the middle rather than along the sides. Trim 2 rust print inner border strips to this length. Stitch 1 of these to each side of the quilt.

2. Measure the width of the quilt top, measuring through the middle rather than along the sides. Trim 2 rust print inner border strips to this length. Stitch to the top and bottom of the quilt.

3. Measure the length of the quilt top, measuring through the middle rather than along the sides. Trim 2 tan-and-red plaid outer border strips to this length. Stitch 1 of these to each side of the quilt.

4. Measure the width of the quilt top, measuring through the middle rather than along the sides. Trim 2 tan-and-red plaid outer border strips to this length. Stitch 1 of these to the top and bottom of the quilt.

Quilting and Finishing

1. Mark the desired quilting designs on the quilt top. The quilt shown has outline quilting around the shapes in the Bear's Paw blocks, a double line in the center square of each block, and a cable design in the border.

2. Layer backing, batting, and quilt top. Baste.

3. Quilt as desired.

4. Referring to the general instructions on page 21, make 158" of bias binding and apply to the quilt.

Diagram 1

Diagram 2

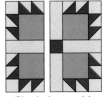

Block Assembly Diagram

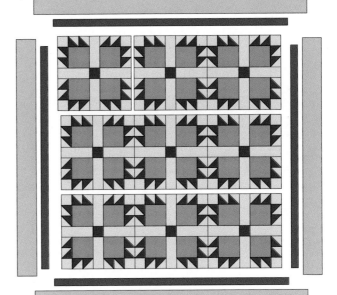

Quilt Top Assembly Diagram

Keyport Shores

Quilt: 31½" x 31½"
Finished Block Size: 6" square

Keyport Shores by Cleo Nollette, 1995, Keyport, Washington. Quilted by the Ohio Amish.

Sometimes a piece of fabric jumps off the shelf and lands in your arms.
Wonderful novelty prints, such as this one with adorable 1920s-style children, give us
many inspirations for quilts. This design is a particularly
good way to showcase large motifs in a novelty print.

Materials

½ to 1 yard of novelty print (Be sure to buy enough to cut out the proper number of design motifs.)

¾ yard cream print for triangles and inner borders

¼ yard each or scraps of red, green, blue, and gold for triangles

⅜ yard red print for outer border

1 yard fabric for backing

¾ yard batting

¼ yard fabric for binding

Cutting

From the *novelty print*, cut:
• 16 (4½") squares.

> *Tip:* Make a window template by cutting a 4½" square in the center of a sheet of paper. You can use the window to frame the area to see where to center your design.

From the *cream print*, cut:
• 16 (6") squares.
• 4 (1½" x 36") strips.

From the *scraps of red, green, blue, and gold*, cut:
• 16 (6") squares (4 for each block).
• 16 (1½" x 12") strips (4 for each block). Cut the strips into 1½" x 2½" pieces.

From the *red print*, cut:
• 4 (3" x 36") strips.

Assembling the Blocks

1. Referring to the general instructions for making squares from half-square triangles on pages 55–56, use the 6" squares of cream and red, green, blue, and gold to make 192 (1½") half-square triangle units (48 of each color scheme) as follows:
• Cut the bias strips 1¾".
• Cut the segments 1½".
• Cut the squares 1½".

2. Referring to Block Assembly Diagram, arrange the pieces for each block as shown.

3. Join the pieces into 3 vertical rows; then join rows as shown in the Block Diagram. Make 16 blocks.

Assembling the Quilt

1. Join the blocks in 4 horizontal rows of 4 blocks each as shown in the Quilt Top Assembly Diagram. Pin and carefully sew all match points.

2. Join the rows to form the quilt top.

Borders

1. Measure the length of the quilt top, measuring through the middle rather than along the sides. Trim 2 cream print inner border strips to this length. Stitch 1 of these to each side of the quilt.

2. Measure the width of the quilt top, measuring through the middle rather than along the sides. Trim 2 cream print inner border strips to this length. Stitch to the top and bottom of the quilt.

3. Measure the length of the quilt top, measuring through the middle rather than along the sides. Trim 2 red print outer border strips to this length. Stitch to each side of the quilt.

4. Measure the width of the quilt top, measuring through the middle rather than along the sides. Trim 2 red print outer border strips to this length. Stitch to the top and bottom of the quilt.

Quilting and Finishing

1. Mark the desired quilting designs on the quilt top. The quilt shown has outline quilting around the shapes in the novelty print and triangles in the blocks, and a spiral design in the border.

2. Layer backing, batting, and quilt top. Baste.

3. Quilt as desired.

4. Referring to the general instructions on page 21, make 126" of bias binding and apply to the quilt.

Block Assembly Diagram

Block Diagram

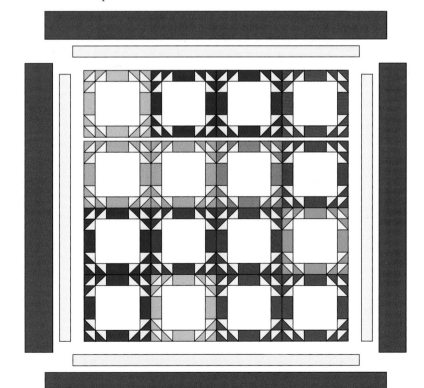

Quilt Top Assembly Diagram

Miniature Hens and Chicks

Quilt: 24" x 24"
Finished Block Size: 5" square

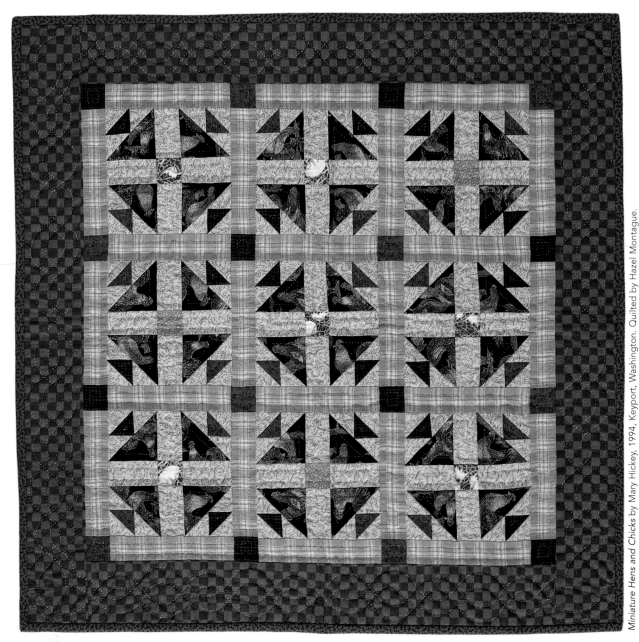

Miniature Hens and Chicks by Mary Hickey, 1994, Keyport, Washington. Quilted by Hazel Montague.

This traditional block features several chicken prints. The plaid sashing

and the red-and-green triangles and squares add exuberance to this cheerful

miniature. Since the block pieces are so small, look for a novelty

print with motifs that are small enough to show when cut.

Materials

1 yard light print for background

¼ yard black chicken print for large triangles

¼ yard red print for small triangles, sashing squares, and border

¼ yard green print for small triangles and sashing squares

¼ yard gold plaid for sashing

¼ yard or scrap of dark gold for block centers

¾ yard fabric for backing

¾ yard batting

⅝ yard fabric for binding

Cutting

From the *light print*, cut:

• 3 (1½" x 42") strips. Cut the strips into 36 (1½" x 2½") pieces.

• 2 (1⅞" x 42") strips. Cut the strips into 36 (1⅞") squares. Cut the squares in half diagonally to make 72 triangles.

• 2 (9") squares.

From the *black chicken print*, cut:

• 2 (2⅞" x 42") strips. Cut the strips into 18 (2⅞") squares. Cut the squares in half diagonally to make 36 triangles.

From the *red print*, cut:

• 1 (9") square.

• 1 (1½" x 20") strip. Cut the strip into 8 (1½") squares.

• 4 (2¾"-wide) strips for borders.

From the *green print*, cut:

• 1 (9") square.

• 1 (1½" x 20") strip. Cut the strip into 8 (1½") squares.

From the *dark gold*, cut:

• 1 (1½" x 20") strip. Cut the strip into 9 (1½") squares.

From the *gold plaid*, cut:

• 4 (1½" x 42") strips. Cut the strips into 24 (1½" x 5½") pieces.

Assembling the Blocks

1. Referring to the general instructions for making squares from half-square triangles on pages 55–56, use the 9" squares of light print, red print, and green print to make 18 (1½") half-square triangle squares each of red and green as follows:

• Cut the bias strips 1¾".

• Cut the segments 1½".

• Cut the squares 1½".

2. Referring to the Block Assembly Diagram, arrange the pieces for each block as shown.

3. Join the pieces into 3 vertical rows; then join rows as shown in Block Diagram. Make 9 blocks.

Assembling the Quilt

1. Join 3 gold plaid sashing pieces, alternating a red or green square between each piece and on each end of the row. Make 4 sashing rows as shown in Quilt Top Assembly Diagram.

2. Join 3 blocks into a row with a sashing piece between the blocks and on each end of the row. Make 3 block rows as shown in Quilt Top Assembly Diagram.

3. Join the block rows with a sashing row between each row.

4. Join a sashing row to the top and bottom of the quilt as shown.

Borders

1. Measure the length of the quilt top, measuring through the middle rather than along the sides. Trim 2 red print border strips to this length. Stitch 1 of these to each side of the quilt.

2. Measure the width of the quilt top, measuring through the middle rather than along the sides. Trim 2 red print border strips to this length. Stitch 1 of these to the top and bottom of the quilt.

Quilting and Finishing

1. Mark the desired quilting designs on the quilt top. The quilt shown has outline quilting inside the triangles and rectangles of the Hens and Chicks blocks, a double line in each sashing piece and sashing square, and a cable design in the border.

2. Layer backing, batting, and quilt top. Baste.

3. Quilt as desired.

4. Referring to the general instructions on page 21, make 96" of bias binding and apply to the quilt.

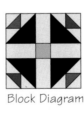

Block Assembly Diagram

Block Diagram

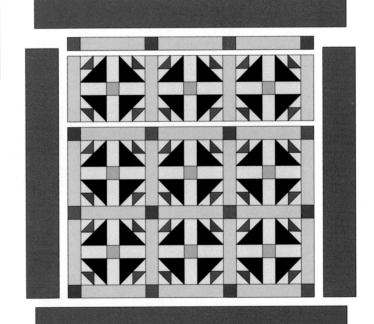

Quilt Top Assembly Diagram

Miniature Maple Leaf

Quilt: 20¼" x 20¼"
Finished Block Size: 3" square

Miniature Maple Leaf by Mary Hickey, 1994, Keyport, Washington. Quilted by Hazel Montague.

Brilliant golden leaves caught in a windy blue sky make this quilt

a stunning accent piece. Use a variety of golds and rusts to paint each leaf with

your fabrics. Appliquéing the slender stems in place eliminates the

problem of piecing tiny elements.

Materials

⅝ yard blue print for background
¼ yard each or scraps of 9 different fabrics for leaves
¼ yard second blue print for setting pieces
¼ yard gold for inner border
¼ yard dark blue for outer border
¾ yard fabric for backing
¾ yard batting
½ yard fabric for binding

Cutting

From the *blue print*, cut:
• 9 (6") squares.
• 9 (1½") squares.
From each of the *scraps for leaves*, cut:
• 1 (6") square.
• 1 (1½") square.
• 1 (1½" x 2½") rectangle.
• 1 (1" x 3") strip.
From the *second blue print*, cut:
• 4 (3½") squares.
• 2 (5¼") squares. Cut squares in quarters diagonally to make 8 side triangles.
• 2 (3½") squares. Cut squares in half diagonally to make 4 corner triangles.
From the *gold*, cut:
• 4 (1¼" x 20") strips for inner border.
From the *dark blue print*, cut:
• 4 (3¼" x 20") strips.

Assembling the Blocks

1. Referring to the general instructions for making squares from half-square triangles on pages 55–56, use the 6" squares of blue and scraps for leaves to make 4 (1½") half-square triangle units of each color as follows:
• Cut the bias strips 1¾".
• Cut the segments 1½".
• Cut the squares 1½".

2. To make a stem, fold each 1" x 3" leaf fabric strip in half lengthwise with wrong sides facing and press (Diagram 1).
3. Fold 1 (1½") blue print square in half diagonally and press a crease, as shown in Diagram 2. Unfold the square.
4. Place 1 folded strip to the right of the crease on 1 blue square, with the raw edge of the strip exactly on the crease. Stitch the strip to the square ⅛" from the raw edges (Diagram 3).
5. Fold the strip over to the left and hand- or machine-stitch along the left edge (Diagram 4). Repeat steps 3–5 for each stem.

6. Arrange the pieces for each block as shown in the *Block Assembly Diagram*.
7. Join the pieces into 3 vertical rows; then join rows as shown in the *Block Diagram*. Repeat to make 9 blocks.

Diagram 1

Diagram 2

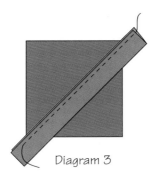

Diagram 3

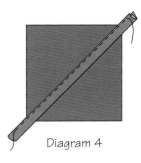

Diagram 4

Block Assembly Diagram

Block Diagram

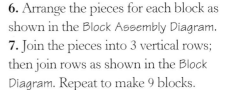

Assembling the Quilt

1. Arrange the blocks and setting pieces in diagonal rows as shown in the *Quilt Top Assembly Diagram.*
2. Join the blocks and setting pieces in diagonal rows.
3. Join the rows to form the quilt top.

Borders

1. Measure the length of the quilt top, measuring through the middle rather than along the sides. Trim 2 gold print inner border strips to this length. Stitch 1 of these to the top and bottom of the quilt.
2. Measure the width of the quilt top, measuring through the middle rather than along the sides. Trim 2 gold print inner border strips to this length. Stitch 1 of these to each end of the quilt.
3. Measure the length of the quilt top, measuring through the middle rather than along the sides. Trim 2 dark blue print outer border strips to this length. Stitch 1 of these to each side of the quilt.
4. Measure the width of the quilt top, measuring through the middle rather than along the sides. Trim 2 dark blue outer border strips to this length. Stitch 1 of these to the top and bottom of the quilt.

Quilting and Finishing

1. Mark the desired quilting designs on the quilt top. The quilt shown has outline quilting in the shapes in the leaf blocks, straight-line quilting in the inner border, and a maple leaf pattern in the outer border.
2. Layer backing, batting, and quilt top. Baste.
3. Quilt as desired.
4. Referring to general instructions on page 21, make 81" of bias binding and apply to the quilt.

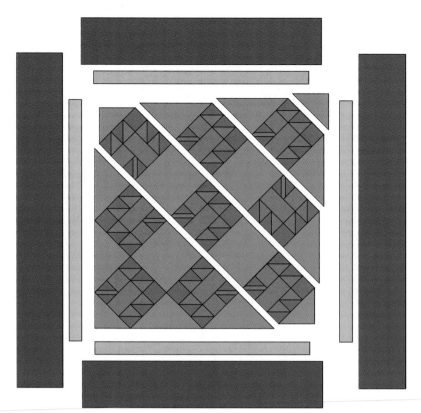

Quilt Top Assembly Diagram

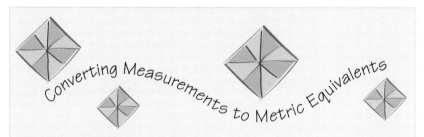

Converting Measurements to Metric Equivalents

For our quilting friends in other lands, here's a helpful hint for converting inches and yards to centimeters and meters.

To find centimeters:
Multiply inches and fractions of inches by 2.54 to find centimeters. For example, ¼" equals .64 cm (.25" x 2.54 = .635 cm) and 3½" equals 8.9 cm (3.5" x 2.54 = 8.89 cm).

To find meters:
Multiply yards and fractions of yards by .9 to find meters. For example, 4⅜ yards equals 3.94 meters (4.375 yards x .9 = 3.938 m).

See page 59 for a handy chart that converts fractions to decimals.

Contrary Wife
and Ornery Husband

Quilt: 38" x 38"
Finished Block Size: 6" square

Contrary Wife and Ornery Husband by Mary Hickey, 1994, Keyport, Washington. Quilted by the Ohio Amish.

When you combine two design blocks, often a pattern appears that is stronger
and more interesting than either of the blocks alone. Here, Contrary Wife
blocks mate with Ornery Husband blocks to create the stunning pattern.

Materials

⅝ yard dark rose prints for triangles

⅝ yard dark green prints for triangles

¼ yard light rose print for squares

¼ yard light green print for squares

1½ yards beige prints for triangles and squares

¼ yard green print for border

¼ yard rose print for border

1¼ yards fabric for backing

1¼ yards batting

⅜ yard fabric for binding

Cutting

From the *dark rose prints*, cut:
- 1 (18" x 20") piece [or 3 (12") squares for a scrappy look].

From the *dark green prints*, cut:
- 1 (18" x 20") piece [or 3 (12") squares for a scrappy look].

From the *light rose print*, cut:
- 2 (2½" x 42") strips. Cut strips into 30 (2½") squares.

From the *light green print*, cut:
- 2 (2½" x 42") strips. Cut strips into 30 (2½") squares.

From the *beige prints*, cut:
- 2 (18" x 20") pieces [or 6 (12") squares for a scrappy look].
- 5 (2½" x 42") strips. Cut the strips into 65 (2½") squares.

From the *green border print*, cut:
- 2 (4¼" x 42") strips.

From the *rose border print*, cut:
- 2 (4¼" x 42") strips.

Assembling the Blocks

1. Referring to the general instructions for making half-square triangles on pages 55–56, use the 18" x 20" pieces of green and beige to make 50 (2½") half-square triangle units as follows:
- Cut the bias strips 2½".
- Cut the segments 2½".
- Cut the squares 2½".

2. Referring to the general instructions for making half-square triangles on pages 55–56, use the 18" x 20" pieces of rose and beige to make 50 (2½") half-square triangle units as follows:
- Cut the bias strips 2½".
- Cut the segments 2½".
- Cut the squares 2½".

3. Referring to *Block Diagrams*, arrange the pieces for each block as shown. Make 6 of Block 1, 6 of Block 2, and 13 of Block 3.

Assembling the Quilt

1. Arrange the blocks in 5 horizontal rows of 5 blocks each, as shown in *Quilt Top Assembly Diagram*.

2. Join the blocks in each row, and then join the rows to form the quilt top.

Contrary Wife Blocks

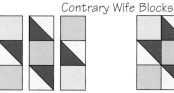

Block 1 Assembly Diagram

Block 1 Diagram Make 6.

Block 2 Assembly Diagram

Block 2 Diagram Make 6.

Ornery Husband Blocks

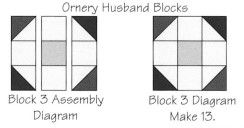

Block 3 Assembly Diagram

Block 3 Diagram Make 13.

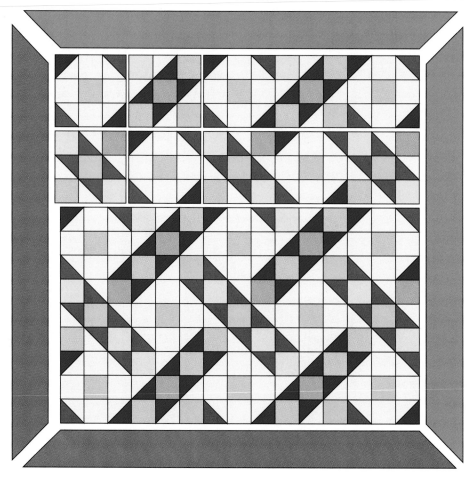

Quilt Top Assembly Diagram

Borders

1. See general instructions on page 16 for tips on mitered border construction.
2. Stitch the borders to the quilt top, mitering corners.

Quilting and Finishing

1. Mark the desired quilting designs on the quilt top. The quilt shown has straight-line quilting along the arrow shape, a leaf scroll in the Ornery Husband blocks (Block 3), and a curved pattern in the outer border.

2. Layer backing, batting, and quilt top. Baste.
3. Quilt as desired.
4. Referring to the general instructions on page 21, make 152" of bias binding and apply to the quilt.

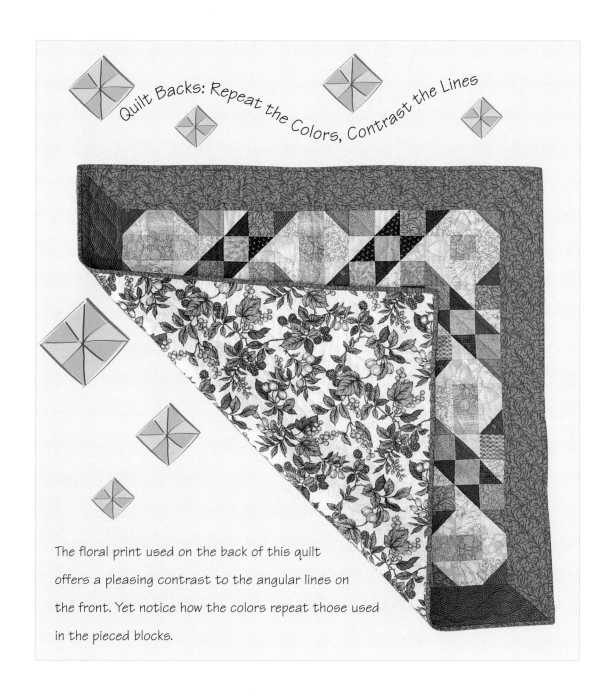

Quilt Backs: Repeat the Colors, Contrast the Lines

The floral print used on the back of this quilt offers a pleasing contrast to the angular lines on the front. Yet notice how the colors repeat those used in the pieced blocks.

Miniature Churn Dash

Quilt: 17³/₄" x 17³/₄"
Finished Block Size: 2³/₄" square

Some fabrics come with charming border prints that we're not sure what to do with.
You only need a few short pieces to make this fun miniature. Pick colors to coordinate with
a border print you like and churn out a batch of tiny Churn Dash blocks.

Materials

⅜ yard muslin for block backgrounds
¼ yard light green print for squares
⅜ yard red print for triangles
⅜ yard gold print for block centers, setting squares, and setting triangles
¾ yard fabric for border
¾ yard fabric for backing
¾ yard batting
½ yard fabric for binding

Cutting

From the *muslin,* cut:
• 4 (1" x 20") strip.
• 1 (9") square.
From the *light green print,* cut:
• 4 (1" x 20") strips.
From the *red print,* cut:
• 1 (9") square.
From the *gold print,* cut:
• 1 (1¼" x 20") strip.
• 4 (3¼") squares.
• 2 (5") squares. Cut the squares in quarters diagonally to make 8 side triangles.
• 2 (3¼") squares. Cut the squares in half diagonally to make 4 corner triangles.
From the *border fabric,* cut:
• 4 (3¼" x 18") strips.

Assembling the Blocks

1. Sew strip sets as shown in Strip Set Diagrams:
• 1 of Strip Set A—muslin/green/gold /green/muslin. Cut 9 (1¼"-wide) segments from Strip Set A.
• 2 of Strip Set B—muslin/green. Cut 18 (1¼"-wide) segments from Strip Set B.
2. Referring to the general instructions for making squares from half-square triangles on pages 55–56, use the 9" squares of muslin and red to make 36 (1½") half-square triangle units as follows:
• Cut the bias strips 1¾".
• Cut the segments 1½".
• Cut the squares 1½".
3. Arrange the pieces for each block as shown in the Block Assembly Diagram.
4. Join the pieces into 3 vertical rows; then join rows as shown in the Block Diagram. Make 9 blocks.

Assembling the Quilt

1. Arrange the blocks and setting squares in diagonal rows as shown in the Quilt Top Assembly Diagram.
2. Join the blocks and setting squares in diagonal rows.
3. Join the rows to form the quilt top.

Borders

1. See general instructions on page 16 for tips on making mitered borders.
2. Stitch the borders to the quilt top, mitering corners.

Quilting and Finishing

1. Mark the desired quilting designs on the quilt top. The quilt shown has outline quilting around the shapes in the Churn Dash blocks, hearts in each setting square and triangle, and outline quilting around the birdhouses.
2. Layer backing, batting, and quilt top. Baste.
3. Quilt as desired.
4. Referring to the general instructions on page 21, make 71" of bias binding and apply to the quilt.

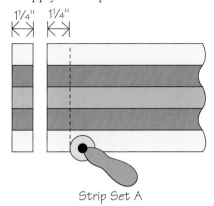

Strip Set A

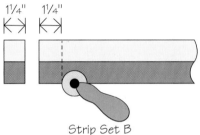

Strip Set B

Block Assembly Diagram   Block Diagram

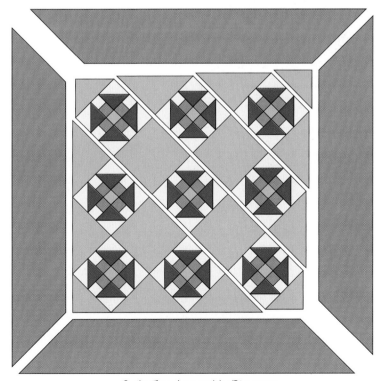

Quilt Top Assembly Diagram

Carolina Rose, page 94.

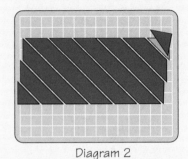

Quilts Made with Quarter-Square Triangles

Piecing small quarter-square triangles can be tedious, and it is easy to stretch

their bias edges out of shape. My shortcut method eliminates these problems.

You don't even need to cut triangles to make them!

In the previous chapter, you learned a shortcut method for making pieced squares from half-square triangle units. If you cut this completed square across the diagonal, you get even smaller units called quarter-square triangles. When reassembled, the triangles become squares again, called quarter-square units.

1. Cut one rectangular piece from each of two different fabrics.

2. Stack fabrics right side up.

3. With the fabrics layered, position ruler with 45°-angle line along the bottom of the fabric. Make a diagonal cut near the corner (Diagram 1).

4. Cut strips parallel to the initial diagonal cut (Diagram 2). The strips must be cut ⅞" wider than the finished square. Each set of quilt instructions will tell you how wide to cut the strips.

5. Arrange the two sets of strips as shown in Diagram 3, alternating the colors as shown.

6. Sew the strips into two separate bias strip sets, offsetting the tops ¼" as shown in Diagram 4. Press all seams toward the darker color. The resulting strip set should resemble Diagram 5.

7. Position your square ruler with the 45°-angle line on one of the seams. Align a rectangular ruler with the edge of the square ruler, covering the uneven fabric edges on left. Remove the square ruler. Trim the edge to a perfect 45°-angle with the seams to clean up the left edge (Diagram 6).

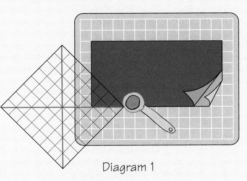

Diagram 1

Diagram 2

Diagram 3

Diagram 4

Diagram 5

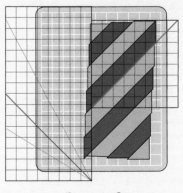

Diagram 6

8. Cut a segment ⅞" wider than the finished square. Each set of quilt instructions will tell you how wide to cut the segment (Diagram 7).

9. Working with one cut segment, place a square ruler with the edge of the ruler on the cut edge of the fabric and the diagonal line on the seam line as shown in Diagram 8. Cut on the right side of the ruler.

10. Position the ruler in the same manner on each seam line and cut, making rectangles (Diagram 9).

11. Turn the cut pieces around so that the untrimmed edges are on the right. Reposition the ruler with the edge of the ruler on the fabric and the diagonal line on the seam, and cut (Diagram 10).

12. Before you cut another segment from the strip unit, be certain to place the ruler with the diagonal line on the seam line and trim the edge to a perfect 45°-angle with the seam line.

13. Cut each square in half diagonally across the seam (Diagram 11).

14. Rearrange the pieces so that the colors are in the right positions.

15. Sew the pairs together to create the squares made of four triangles (Diagram 12).

16. Check to be sure the sewn square is exactly ½" larger than the finished size (Diagram 13).

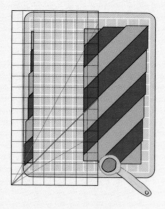

Diagram 7

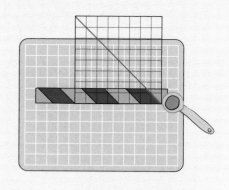

Diagram 8

Diagram 9

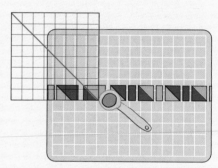

Diagram 10

Diagram 11

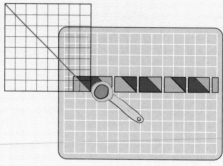

Diagram 12

Diagram 13

Americana Star

Quilt: 41½" x 41½"
Finished Block Size: 7 ½" square

The copper plate-style print in the setting blocks of this quilt gives it an
old-fashioned look. Alternating color schemes in the stars adds interest without
sacrificing the subtle simplicity of the design. The on-point block
setting showcases the star blocks and the print used in the alternate setting pieces.

Materials

¼ yard red print for stars

1 yard navy floral print for stars and outer border

⅝ yard muslin for block background

¼ yard dark red print for block centers

¼ yard navy plaid for block centers

¼ yard light red print for block corners

¼ yard light navy print for block corners

¾ yard blue-and-beige toile for setting pieces

¼ yard red plaid for inner border

1¼ yards fabric for backing

1¼ yards batting

⅜ yard fabric for binding

Cutting

From the *red print*, cut:

• 1 (9" x 20") piece for the star points.

From the *navy floral print*, cut:

• 1 (18" x 20") piece for the star points.

• 4 (3¾" x 42") strips for the outer border.

From the *muslin*, cut:

• 1 (9" x 20") piece for the star backgrounds.

• 1 (18" x 20") piece for the star backgrounds.

From the *dark red print*, cut:

• 1 (3" x 18") strip. Cut the strip into 4 (3") squares for the star block centers.

From the *navy plaid*, cut:

• 1 (3" x 18") strip. Cut the strip into 5 (3") squares for the star block centers.

From the *light red print*, cut:

• 2 (3" x 42") strips. Cut the strips into 16 (3") squares for the star block corners.

From the *light navy print*, cut:

• 2 (3" x 42") strips. Cut the strips into 20 (3") squares for the star block corners.

From the *blue-and-beige toile*, cut:

• 4 (8") squares for the setting blocks.

• 2 (11½") squares. Cut the squares in quarters diagonally for the side setting triangles.

• 2 (6½") squares. Cut these squares in half diagonally for the corner triangles.

From the *red plaid*, cut:

• 4 (1¾" x 42") strips for the inner border.

Assembling the Blocks

1. Referring to the general instructions for making quarter-square triangles on pages 87–88, use the 9" x 20" pieces of the red print and muslin and the 18" x 20" pieces of the navy floral print and muslin to make 16 red-and-muslin and 20 navy-and-muslin quarter-square triangle units as follows:

• Cut the bias strips 3½".

• Cut the segments 3½".

• Cut the half-square units 3½".

• Cut the half-square units in half diagonally and sew the resulting halves together to make the quarter-square units. Trim the quarter-square units to 3" squares.

2. Arrange the pieces for each block as shown in the Block Assembly Diagrams.

Join the pieces into horizontal rows; then join rows to complete the block (Block Diagrams). Make 4 red star blocks and 5 navy star blocks.

Assembling the Quilt

1. Arrange the blocks and setting pieces into diagonal rows as shown in the Quilt Top Assembly Diagram.

2. Join the rows together to complete the quilt top.

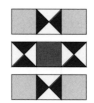

Block Assembly Diagrams

Block Diagrams

Quilt Top Assembly Diagram

Borders

1. Measure the length of the quilt top, measuring through the middle rather than along the sides. Trim 2 red plaid inner border strips to this length. Stitch 1 of these to each side of the quilt.

2. Measure the width of the quilt, measuring through the middle rather than along the ends. Trim 2 red plaid inner border strips to this length. Stitch 1 of these to the top and bottom of the quilt.

3. Measure the length of the quilt top, measuring through the middle rather than along the sides. Trim 2 navy floral print outer border strips to this length. Stitch 1 of these to each side of the quilt.

4. Measure the width of the quilt, measuring through the middle rather than along the ends. Trim 2 navy floral print outer border strips to this length. Stitch 1 of these to the top and bottom of the quilt.

Quilting and Finishing

1. Mark the desired quilting designs on the quilt top. The quilt shown has a diagonal grid quilted throughout the blocks and setting pieces. A curved design is quilted in the border.

2. Layer backing, batting, and quilt top. Baste.

3. Quilt as desired.

4. Referring to the general instructions on page 21, make 166" of bias binding and apply to the quilt.

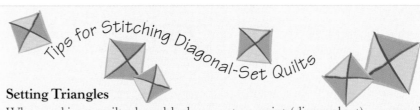

Tips for Stitching Diagonal-Set Quilts

Setting Triangles

When making a quilt whose blocks are set on point (diagonal set), you need setting triangles along the quilt sides to make the quilt square again before adding the borders. These triangles must have the straight of grain along the long side of the triangle to prevent stretching when you add the borders.

To accomplish this, cut squares the finished size of the block x 1.414, plus 1¼". That is, if the finished size of the block in your quilt is 6", multiply 6" x 1.414, which is 8.484 rounded to 8½". Then add 1¼", which is 9¾". Cut the square 9¾". Then cut the square into quarters diagonally to make four triangles. The straight of grain is on the long side of the triangles.

Notching

The side of the setting triangle that is to be sewn to the blocks of a diagonally set quilt has a bias edge. To prevent stretching and for accuracy, mark the triangle to fit the size of the block to which it will be sewn.

When the setting triangles are still on the cutting table, starting at the right-angle corner, measure and mark the size of the unfinished block. That is, if the finished block is 6", the unfinished size is 6½". Make a small mark with a pencil at this point (photo A). Make a small clip with scissors at the mark (photo B). Do not cut off the point; just make a little clip. Do this on both bias sides (or legs) of the triangle.

When sewing the setting triangle to the block, the raw edge of the block will match from the right angle corner to the small clip or notch. The point that extends is the seam allowance for the border, which will be added later.

Corners

On a diagonally set quilt, it is easier to sew on a corner that is bigger than needed and then trim it to size. Cut a square about 1" larger that the finished-size of the block. Cut the square in half diagonally to make two triangles. This will put the straight of the grain on the short sides (or legs) of the triangle, on the outer edge of the quilt.

Sew the triangle to the corner, even if it is too big. Press the seam toward the triangle. Using a large triangle or ruler, line up the edges and trim the corner to size. Be sure not to cut off the seam allowances needed for the border.

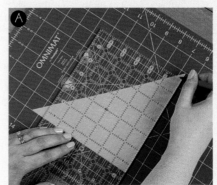
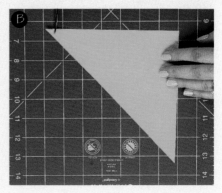

Elizabethan Star

Quilt: 32½" x 32½"
Finished Block Size: 7 ½" square

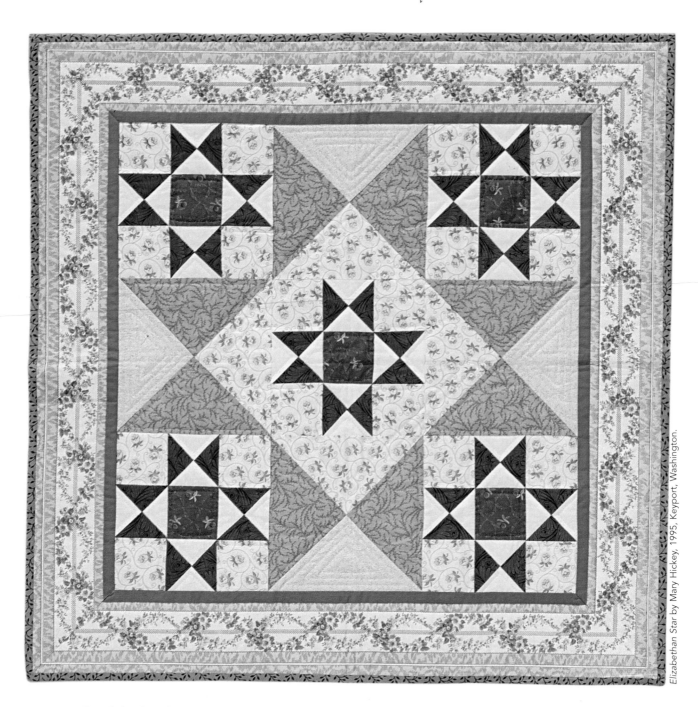

Elizabethan Star by Mary Hickey, 1995, Keyport, Washington.

Careful color placement in the four Hourglass setting blocks creates a large but subtle star to echo the five small Ohio Stars. Look for a lovely floral stripe and then match the star colors to the stripe. Don't be afraid to use strong versions of some of the colors in the stripe.

Materials

½ yard white for star block backgrounds
½ yard rust print for star block triangles
⅛ yard green print for star block centers
⅝ yard floral print for star block corners and Hourglass triangles
½ yard medium peach print for Hourglass triangles
½ yard light peach print for Hourglass triangles
¼ yard dark green print for inner border
⅝ yard floral stripe for outer border
1¼ yards fabric for backing
1¼ yards batting
⅜ yard fabric for binding

Cutting

From the *white*, cut:
• 1 (18" x 20") strip for the star block backgrounds.

From the *rust print*, cut:
• 1 (18" x 20") strip for star block triangles.

From the *green print*, cut:
• 1 (3" x 18") strip. Cut the strip into 5 (3") squares for the star block centers.

From the *floral print* for star block, cut:
• 2 (3" x 42") strips. Cut the strips into 20 (3") squares for the star block corners.
• 1 (8¾") square. Cut the square in quarters diagonally for the Hourglass triangles.

From the *medium peach print*, cut:
• 2 (8¾") squares. Cut the squares in quarters diagonally for the Hourglass triangles.

From the *light peach print* for Hourglass blocks, cut:
• 1 (8¾") square. Cut the square in quarters diagonally for the Hourglass triangles.

From the *dark green print*, cut:
• 4 (1" x 42") strips for the inner border.

From the *floral stripe*, cut:
• 4 (4¾" x 42") strips for the outer border.

Assembling the Blocks

1. Referring to the general instructions for making quarter-square triangles on pages 87–88, use the 18" x 20" pieces of white and rust to make 20 quarter-square triangle units as follows:
• Cut the bias strips 3½".
• Cut the segments 3½".
• Cut the half-square units 3½".
• Cut the half-square units in half diagonally and sew the resulting halves together to make the quarter-square units. Trim the quarter-square units to 3" squares.

2. Arrange the pieces for each star block as shown in *Block 1 Assembly Diagram*. Join the pieces into horizontal rows; then join rows to complete the block (*Block 1 Diagram*). Make 5 blocks.

3. Arrange the pieces for each Hourglass block as shown in the *Block 2 Assembly Diagram*. Join the pieces along the diagonal to complete the block (*Block 2 Diagram*). Make 4 blocks.

Assembling the Quilt

1. Join the blocks in 3 horizontal rows of 3 blocks each as shown in the *Quilt Top Assembly Diagram*.

2. Join the rows together to complete the quilt top.

Borders

1. See the general instructions on page 16 for tips on mitered borders.

2. Stitch the borders to the quilt top, mitering corners.

Quilting and Finishing

1. Mark the desired quilting designs on the quilt top. The quilt shown has outline quilting around the shapes in the star blocks, a double line in each Hourglass triangle. and a cable design in the border.

2. Layer backing, batting, and quilt top. Baste.

3. Quilt as desired.

4. Referring to the general instructions on page 21, make 148" of bias binding and apply to quilt.

Block 1 Assembly Diagram   Block 1 Diagram

Block 2 Assembly Diagram   Block 2 Diagram

Quilt Top Assembly Diagram

Carolina Rose

Quilt: 38½" x 38½"
Finished Block Size: 7 ½" square

Carolina Rose by Mary Hickey, 1995, Keyport, Washington. Quilted by the Ohio Amish.

This quilt's simple color scheme is reminiscent of 19th century

"best quilt" style. Generous hand quilting creates a stunning wall hanging.

The tiny triangles are easy to piece using my method for quarter-square triangles.

The Celtic Knot quilting design softens the inner border of sawtooth triangles.

Materials

2 yards muslin for background
1 yard solid red for block, sawtooth border triangles, and outer border
¼ yard red stripe for flower
¼ yard green print for base of flower and center square
1¼ yards fabric for backing
1¼ yards batting
⅜ yard fabric binding

Cutting

Make a template for the wedge shape on page 96.

From the *muslin,* cut:
• 1 (18" x 20") piece for block triangles.
• 3 (18" x 20") pieces for sawtooth border triangles.
• 5 (2" x 42") strips. Cut 2 of the strips into 36 (2") squares for the flower background. Cut 3 of the strips into 36 (2" x 3½") pieces for flower background.
• 4 (8") squares for setting blocks.
• 2 (12") squares. Cut the squares in quarters diagonally to make 8 side setting triangles.
• 2 (7") squares. Cut the squares in half diagonally to make 4 corner triangles.

From the *solid red,* cut:
• 1 (18" x 20") piece for the flower triangles.
• 3 (18" x 20") pieces for the sawtooth border triangles.
• 4 (3¼" x 42") strips for the outer border.

From the *red stripe,* cut:
• 2 (3⅞"-wide) strips. Cut the strips into 18 (3⅞") squares. Cut the squares in half diagonally. Place the template on the triangles as shown in Diagram 1 and trim off the corners.

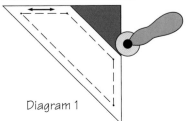

Diagram 1

From the *green print,* cut:
• 1 (2⅜"-wide) strip. Cut the strip into 18 (2⅜") squares. Cut the squares in half diagonally to make the bases of the flowers.
• 1 (2" x 42") strip. Cut the strip into 9 (2") squares for the block centers.

Assembling the Blocks

1. Referring to the general instructions for making quarter-square triangles on pages 87–88, use the 18" x 20" pieces of muslin and solid red to make 72 quarter-square triangle units as follows:
• Cut the bias strips 2⅜".
• Cut the segments 2⅜".
• Cut the half-square units 2⅜".
• Cut the half-square units in half diagonally. Set aside for the blocks.

2. Referring to the general instructions for making half-square triangles on pages 55–56, use the 18" x 20" pieces of muslin and solid red for the

sawtooth border triangles to make 92 (3½") half-square triangles blocks as follows:
• Cut the bias strips 2".
• Cut the segments 2".
• Cut the squares 2".

Block Assembly Diagram   Block Diagram

3. Arrange the pieces for each block as shown in the Block Assembly Diagram. Join the pieces into vertical rows; then join rows to complete the block (Block Diagram). Make 9 blocks.

Assembling the Quilt

1. Join the blocks and setting pieces in diagonal rows as shown in the Quilt Top Assembly Diagram.
2. Join the rows together to complete the quilt top. ·····················➤

Quilt Top Assembly Diagram

 Carolina Rose   95

Borders

1. Stitch 2 borders of 22 half-square triangles each, as shown in *Diagram 2*. Stitch 1 of these to each side of the quilt.

2. Stitch 2 borders of 24 half-square triangles each, as shown is *Diagram 3*. Stitch 1 of these to the top and bottom of the quilt.

3. Measure the length of the quilt top, measuring through the middle rather than along the sides. Trim 2 solid red outer border strips to this length. Stitch 1 of these to each side of the quilt.

4. Measure the width of the quilt top, measuring through the middle rather than along the sides. Trim 2 solid red outer border strips to this length. Stitch 1 of these to the top and bottom of the quilt.

Quilting and Finishing

1. Mark the desired quilting designs on the quilt top. The quilt shown has outline quilting ¼" inside and outside around the shapes in the Carolina Rose blocks and the Sawtooth border, a double line Celtic Knot in the setting blocks, and a cable design in the border.

2. Layer backing, batting, and quilt top. Baste.

3. Quilt as desired.

4. Referring to the general instructions on page 21, make 162" of bias binding and apply to the quilt.

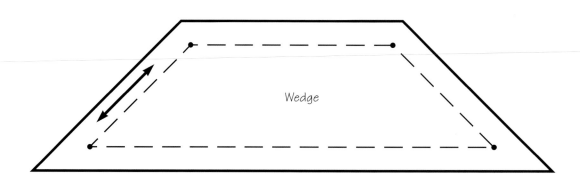

Diagram 2

Diagram 3

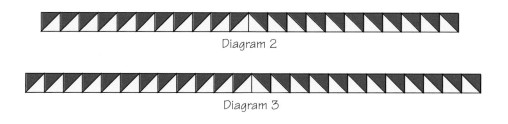

Wedge

Searching for the Perfect Quilting Design

There are books available with Celtic Knot designs, as well as ready-made plastic quilting stencils. I like to collect these designs and use them in large, open areas of my quilts, as in *Carolina Rose*.

Garden Star

Quilt: 35" x 43½"
Finished Block Size: 6" square

Garden Star by Cleo Nollette, 1995, Seattle, Washington.

A garden of scrappy pastel stars blooms in a field of vines and flowers.

These delicate stars are easy to make when you know how to speed-piece the

little triangles. So get out your pastel prints and plant a garden of stars.

Materials

4 (9") squares (⅓ yard) white for star
  block backgrounds
4 (9") squares assorted medium prints
  for star points
Scraps totaling ¼ yard in assorted pastels for block corner squares
1 yard light floral print for block
  centers and setting triangles
¼ yard green print for inner border
½ yard large floral print for outer
  border
1¼ yards fabric for backing
1¼ yards batting
⅜ yard fabric for binding

Cutting

From the *assorted pastels,* cut:
• 44 (2½") squares for star background
  corners.
From the *light floral print,* cut:
• 11 (2½") squares for star centers.
• 4 (5½") squares. Cut the squares in
  half diagonally for corner setting
  triangles on Rows 1 and 3.
• 5 (9⅜") squares. Cut the squares in
  quarters diagonally for the side setting triangles.
• 1 (9¾") square. Cut the square in half
  diagonally for top and bottom setting triangles in Row 2.
From the *green print,* cut:
• 4 (1¼" x 42") strips for the inner
  border.
From the *large floral print,* cut:
• 4 (4¼" x 42") strips.

Assembling the Blocks

1. Referring to the general instructions
for making quarter-square triangles on
pages 87–88, use the 9" squares of
white and assorted pastels to make
quarter-square triangle units as follows:
• Cut the bias strips 3".
• Cut the segments 3".
• Cut the half-square units 3".
• Cut the half-square units in half diagonally and sew the resulting halves
together to make 44 quarter-square

units. Trim the quarter-square units to
2½" square.
2. Arrange the pieces for each block as
shown in the *Block Assembly Diagram.*
Join the pieces into horizontal rows;
then join rows to complete the block
(*Block Diagram*). Make 11 blocks.

Block Assembly Diagram

Assembling the Quilt

1. Arrange the blocks and setting
pieces into 2 vertical rows with 4
blocks in Rows 1 and 3 and with 3
blocks in Row 2, as shown in the *Quilt
Top Assembly Diagram.*
2. Join the rows together to complete
the quilt top.

Block Diagram

Quilt Top Assembly Diagram

Borders

1. Measure the length of the quilt top, measuring through the middle rather than along the sides. Trim 2 green print inner border strips to this length. Stitch 1 of these to each side of the quilt.

2. Measure the width of the quilt top, measuring through the middle rather than along the sides. Trim 2 green print inner border strips to this length. Stitch 1 of these to the top and bottom of the quilt.

3. Measure the length of the quilt top, measuring through the middle rather than along the sides. Trim 2 large floral print outer border strips to this length. Stitch 1 of these to each side of the quilt.

4. Measure the width of the quilt top, measuring through the middle rather than along the sides. Trim 2 large floral print outer border strips to this length. Stitch 1 of these to the top and bottom of the quilt.

Quilting and Finishing

1. Mark the desired quilting designs on the quilt top. The quilt shown has outline quilting around the shapes in the star blocks, a double line in each setting piece, and a cable design in the border.

2. Layer backing, batting, and quilt top. Baste.

3. Quilt as desired.

4. Referring to the general instructions on page 21, make 157" of bias binding and apply to the quilt.

How to Preserve and Care for Small Quilts

A quilt's greatest enemies are light and dirt. Since it is nearly impossible to completely avoid these two problems, you might want to take the following suggestions into account.

Prevent Fading

A quilt on display is bound to fade over time. However, you can limit fading by hanging your quilt on a wall that does not receive direct sunlight. To extend the life of a quilt that must hang on a wall that's exposed to a window, try rotating it with other quilts throughout the year.

When a quilt is not in use, store it in a cotton pillowcase. Avoid using plastic bags, which tend to trap moisture and can cause your quilt to mildew. This problem is especially common in high-humidity climates.

Washing

Small quilts will not receive the same wear and tear as bed quilts, so you should not have to clean them often. You can vacuum wall quilts to remove dust and pet hair. Avoid dry cleaning—it leaves harmful chemicals in the fibers that can discolor your quilt over time.

Sometimes a good airing is all that's needed to freshen a quilt. Hanging your quilts outside on a clear spring day can often get rid of any stale odors.

When you must wash a quilt, use a mild soap such as Ensure or Orvis Paste (a shampoo originally designed for livestock). These soaps are available at quilt shops and from mail-order companies.

When the affected area is small, try spot-cleaning with a bit of soap on a damp washcloth. If the entire quilt needs to be cleaned, wash it by hand in the sink with lukewarm water (use cold water if the quilt has reds or other colors that might bleed). Immerse the quilt and gently agitate it with your hands to disperse the soap. Let it soak for about 10 minutes; then drain the sink.

Squeeze as much water out of the quilt as possible, but don't wring or twist the quilt because this puts undue stress on the stitches and fabric. Rinse the quilt as often as necessary to get rid of all the soap.

Let the quilt dry flat on a towel. If you've used cotton batting and want the quilt to get a puffy, antique look along the stitching, toss it in the dryer on the gentle cycle.

Bow Ties, page 108.

Quilts Made with Diagonal Corners

The diagonal-corners method is a quick and easy alternative to adding tiny triangles to larger

pieces. Some traditional blocks that usually require set-in piecing, like Bow Ties

(pictured at left), can be finished in half the time using the diagonal-corners method.

It's much easier to cut and sew squares and rectangles than triangles. So resourceful quiltmakers developed a method of cutting and sewing squares and rectangles to make triangles. Instead of sewing the long outer edges of triangles together, you sew squares from corner to corner. This method is called the "diagonal-corners" or "diagonal-seams" method. If you've never tried this technique, you can experiment with the quilts in this chapter.

1. With wrong sides facing, fold a square in half diagonally and press a crease (Diagram 1) or draw a pencil line from corner to corner on the wrong side of the square (Diagram 2).

2. With right sides facing, match two sides of the square with two sides of the base rectangle. Stitch from corner to corner of the square along the crease (Diagram 3).

3. Trim the fabric from the excess diagonal-corner fabric only (not the base rectangle), leaving a ¼" seam allowance. Press the triangle back (Diagram 4).

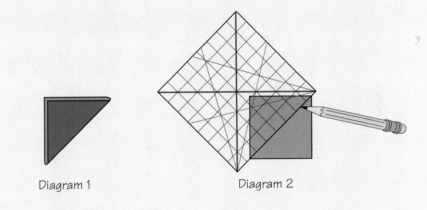

Diagram 1

Diagram 2

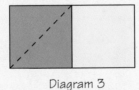

Diagram 3

Diagram 4

Edwardian Star

Quilt: 42" x 42"
Finished Block Size: 6" square

Edwardian Star by Mary Hickey, 1995, Keyport, Washington.

When you buy fabric for this quilt, look for a novelty print whose motifs fit into a 3" space.

Then match the star background to the background of the novelty print

(white in this quilt). Select coordinating colors for the rest of the block. Notice how the

border print ties in all the colors within the quilt top.

Materials

½ yard novelty print for block centers

¼ yard each of 3 or 4 different navy prints for the star points

¼ yard light blue print for block corners

¼ yard yellow print for block corners

⅝ yard bleached muslin for background of star points

¼ yard light gold print for inner border

¼ yard dark gold print for middle border

½ yard royal blue star print for outer border

1⅞ yards fabric for backing

1¼ yards batting

⅜ yard for binding

Cutting

From the *novelty print*, cut:
• 25 (3½") squares for the star centers.

From the *assorted navy prints*, cut:
• 10 (2" x 42") strips. Cut the strips into 200 (2") squares for star points.
• 4 (2") squares for border corners.

From the *light blue print*, cut:
• 3 (2" x 42") strips. Cut the strips into 52 (2") squares for the background corners of 13 blocks.
• 4 (1½") squares for border corners.

From the *yellow print*, cut:
• 3 (2" x 42") strips. Cut the strips into 48 (2") squares for the background corners of 12 blocks.

From the *bleached muslin*, cut:
• 9 (2" x 42") strips. Cut the strips into 100 (2" x 3½") rectangles for background of star points.

From the *light gold print*, cut:
• 4 (1½" x 42") strips for inner borders.

From the *dark gold print*, cut:
• 4 (2" x 42") strips for middle borders.
• 4 (4") squares for border corners.

From the *royal blue star print*, cut:
• 4 (4" x 42") strips for outer borders.

From *backing fabric*, cut:
• 2 (11"-wide) strips. Join these strips end to end. Then join to long side (1¼-yard length) of remaining fabric. Trim excess from pieced end.

Assembling the Blocks

1. With wrong sides facing, fold a 2" navy square in half and press a crease. With right sides facing, match 2 sides of the square with 2 sides of a 2" x 3½" muslin rectangle. Stitch from corner to corner along the crease (Diagram 1).

2. Trim the excess fabric from the diagonal-corner fabric only, leaving a ¼" seam allowance. Place another navy square on the other end of the rectangle and stitch from corner to corner along the crease (Diagram 2).

3. Trim the fabric from the diagonal-corner fabric only, leaving a ¼" seam allowance. Press triangle back (Diagram 3). Repeat with all of the navy squares and muslin rectangles to make 100 star point units.

4. Arrange the pieces for each block as shown in the Block Assembly Diagram. Join the pieces into vertical rows; then join rows to complete block (Block Diagram). Make 13 blocks with blue background corners and 12 blocks with yellow background corners.

Diagram 1

Diagram 2

Diagram 3

Block Assembly Diagram

Block Diagram

Put a Surprise on the Back of Your Quilt!

Vole

Which letter is missing? Inspired by an adorable Edwardian alphabet print, this quilt centers 25 of the letters in the stars on the front of the quilt. The missing letter V is hiding on the back of the quilt. You can put the first letter of your name on the back of the quilt to make a beautiful quilt label.

Assembling the Quilt

1. Join the blocks in 5 horizontal rows of 5 blocks each as shown in *Quilt Top Assembly Diagram*. Pin and carefully sew all match points.

2. Join the rows together to complete the quilt top.

Borders

1. Measure the length of the quilt top, measuring through the middle rather than along the sides. Trim 4 light gold print inner border strips to this length. Stitch 2 of these to the sides of the quilt.

2. Sew the 1¼" light blue squares to the ends of remaining 2 strips. Stitch these to the top and bottom of the quilt.

3. Measure the length of the quilt top, measuring through the middle rather than along the sides. Trim 4 dark gold print middle border strips to this length. Stitch 2 of these to the sides of the quilt.

4. Sew the dark blue squares to the ends of the remaining 2 strips. Stitch these to the top and bottom of the quilt.

5. Measure the length of the quilt top, measuring through the middle rather than along the sides. Trim 4 royal blue star print outer border strips to this length. Stitch 2 of these to the sides of the quilt.

6. Sew the dark gold squares to the ends of the remaining 2 strips. Stitch these to the top and bottom of the quilt.

Quilting and Finishing

1. Mark the desired quilting designs on the quilt top. The quilt shown has outline quilting around the shapes in the stars, circles in the blue-and-yellow four-patch areas, squares in the white background areas, and a cable design in the border.

2. Layer backing, batting, and quilt top. Baste.

3. Quilt as desired.

4. Referring to the general instructions on page 21, make 168" of bias binding and apply to the quilt.

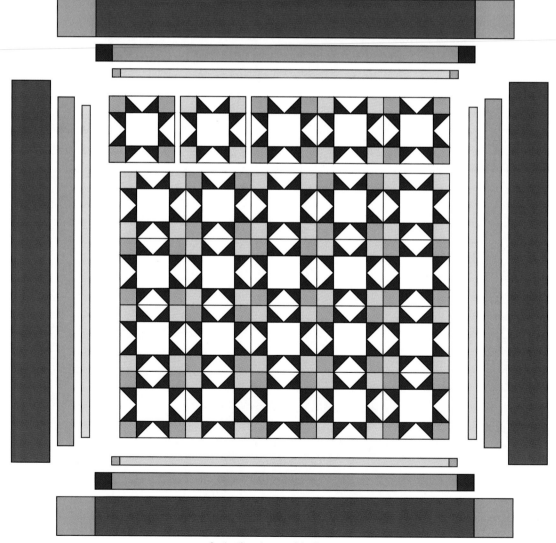

Quilt Top Assembly Diagram

Buttoned Stars

Quilt: 19" x 26"
Finished Block Size: 5" square

Plaids lend playfulness to the stars in this little quilt.

Adding buttons of various sizes enhances the lighthearted mood of the stars.

Materials

¼ yard muslin for background in star blocks

¼ yard or scraps green prints for star triangles [quilt shown uses 3 (1¾"-wide) strips]

¼ yard or scraps red prints for star centers and border

¼ yard red plaid for setting pieces

¾ yard fabric for backing

⅝ yard batting

¼ yard fabric for binding

12 assorted buttons (optional)

Cutting

From the *muslin*, cut:
• 2 (1¾" x 42") strips. Cut strips into 24 (1¾" x 3") rectangles for star backgrounds.
• 1 (1¾" x 42") strip. Cut strip into 24 (1¾") squares for star backgrounds.

From the *green prints*, cut:
• 3 (1¾" x 42") strips. Cut strips into 48 (1¾") squares for star points.

From the *red prints*, cut:
• 6 (3") squares for star centers.
• 4 (2¾" x 42") strips for border.

From the *red plaid*, cut:
• 2 (5½") squares for setting squares.
• 2 (8⅜") squares. Cut squares in quarters diagonally for side setting triangles.
• 2 (4½") squares. Cut squares in half diagonally for the corner triangles.

Assembling the Blocks

1. With wrong sides facing, fold the 1¾" green squares in half and press a crease.

2. With right sides facing, match 2 sides of 1 green square with 2 of the sides of a 1¾" x 3" muslin rectangle. Stitch from corner to corner along the crease (Diagram 1).

Diagram 1

3. Trim the fabric from the diagonal-corner fabric only, leaving a ¼" seam allowance. Press triangle back.

4. Place another green square on the other end of the rectangle and stitch from corner to corner along the crease (Diagram 2). Trim and press.

5. Repeat with all of the green squares and muslin rectangles to make 24 star point units (Diagram 3).

6. Arrange the pieces for each block as

Diagram 2   Diagram 3

shown in the *Block Assembly Diagram*. Join the blocks into vertical rows; then join rows to complete the block (Block Diagram). Make 6 blocks.

Assembling the Quilt

1. Join the blocks and setting pieces in diagonal rows as shown in the *Quilt Top Assembly Diagram*.

2. Join the rows together to complete the quilt top.

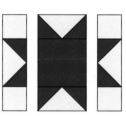

Block Assembly Diagram   Block Diagram

Quilt Top Assembly Diagram

Borders

1. Measure the length of the quilt top, measuring through the middle rather than along the sides. Trim 2 red print border strips to this length. Stitch 1 of these to each side of the quilt.

2. Measure the width of the quilt top, measuring through the middle rather than along the sides. Trim 2 red print border strips to this length. Stitch 1 of these to the top and bottom of the quilt.

Tip: Notice that the border in Julie's quilt is pieced with three different red prints for added visual interest.

Quilting and Finishing

1. Mark the desired quilting designs on the top. The quilt shown has outline quilting around all the shapes in the blocks and a diagonal grid in the setting pieces and border.

2. Layer backing, batting, and quilt top. Baste.

3. Quilt as desired.

4. Referring to the general instructions on page 21, make 90" of bias binding and apply to the quilt.

5. Referring to the photo, embellish the quilt with buttons.

Tip: Did you know that you can add buttons with your sewing machine? All you need is a zigzag setting. Set your stitch length to 0, and tinker with the zigzag setting until the needle rises and falls within your button's holes (turn your wheel by hand while experimenting). Then simply tack the buttons in place with a few stitches!

Stretch Your Imagination for Small Quilts

More Ideas for this Quilt

Christmas Piece

The red-and-green color scheme makes this quilt an especially good choice for Christmas decorating, but the homespun look makes it appropriate for decorating throughout the year.

The quilt is small and can be made so quickly that you might want to make several for Christmas gifts. Look for fabric with small Christmas motifs for the star points. If there is a particular print that you want to showcase, follow the example in *Edwardian Star* and center the motif within the star.

You can use the same pattern to showcase other holiday fabrics, like Easter or Halloween novelty prints.

Button, Button

Has a family member shared her button collection with you, or have you inherited some special buttons? If this quilt will be a gift for that person, you could add a thoughtful touch by using some of those buttons. If there is a history behind your collection, be sure to include that information on the quilt label.

To give this quilt an extra folk look, accent it with wooden buttons. Tie the buttons in place by hand, leaving short thread tails in the button centers. You do not need to use expensive antique buttons. Many craft shops carry inexpensive, unfinished wooden buttons. You can leave the buttons unfinished to enhance the folk look, or paint them to match the fabrics. Or spray varnish on the buttons or stain them to more closely resemble antique pieces.

Tying the Quilt

A quick alternative for finishing some quilts is to tie them with embroidery floss, pearl cotton, or crochet thread. Tying can work well for small quilts because they will not receive the same wear and tear as a bed-sized quilt.

Bow Ties

Quilt: 29½" x 34½"
Finished Block Size: 4" square

Bow Ties by Suzanne Nelson, 1995, Bothell, Washington.

Cheerful faces peek through some of the ties and gather on the border of this quilt.

These Bow Ties feature scraps of fabric in an array of colors to create this lively little quilt.

Materials

½ yard muslin for block background

¼ yard or scraps of reds for Bow Ties

¼ yard or scraps of pinks for Bow Ties

¼ yard or scraps of blues for Bow Ties

⅜ yard or scraps of greens for Bow Ties and inner border

¼ yard or scraps of golds for Bow Ties

1½ yards of theme print for Bow Ties, outer border, and binding

1 yard fabric for backing

1 yard batting

½ yard fabric for binding

Cutting

From the *muslin,* cut:

• 4 (2½" x 42") strips. Cut strips into 60 (2½") squares for background.

From the *reds,* cut:

• 2 (2½" x 18") strips. Cut strips into 12 (2½") squares for Bow Ties.

• 2 (1½" x 18") strips. Cut strips into 12 (1½") squares for Bow Ties.

From the *pinks,* cut:

• 2 (2½" x 18") strips. Cut strips into 8 (2½") squares for Bow Ties.

• 2 (1½" x 18") strips. Cut strips into 8 (1½") squares for Bow Ties.

From the *blues,* cut:

• 2 (2½" x 18") strips. Cut strips into 10 (2½") squares for Bow Ties.

• 2 (1½" x 18") strips. Cut strips into 10 (1½") squares for Bow Ties.

From the *greens,* cut:

• 2 (2½" x 18") strips. Cut strips into 12 (2½") squares for Bow Ties.

• 2 (1½" x 18") strips. Cut strips into 12 (1½") squares for Bow Ties.

• 4 (1¼" x 42") strips for inner borders.

From the *golds,* cut:

• 2 (2½" x 18") strips. Cut strips into 10 (2½") squares for Bow Ties.

• 2 (1½" x 18") strips. Cut strips into 10 (1½") squares for Bow Ties.

From the *theme print,* cut:

• 2 (2½" x 18") strips. Cut strips into 8 (2½") squares for Bow Ties.

• 2 (1½" x 18") strips. Cut strips into 8 (1½") squares for Bow Ties.

• 4 (4¼" x 36") strips for outer borders.

• 1 (22") square for bias binding.

Tip: Notice that the border fabric that Suzanne used is a directional print. To ensure that the little faces are all upright, she cut two crosswise strips and two lengthwise strips.

Assembling the Blocks

1. With wrong sides facing, fold each of the 1½" squares in half diagonally and press a crease (Diagram 1).

2. With right sides facing, place a 1½" square on 1 of the muslin squares. Align 2 of the sides of the colored square with 2 of the sides of the muslin square. Sew along the crease (Diagram 2).

3. Trim the fabric from the diagonal-corner fabric only, leaving ¼" seam allowance. Press triangle back (Diagram 3). Repeat with each pair of colored and muslin squares to make 60 units (30 pairs).

4. Arrange the matching pieces for each Bow Tie as shown in the Block Assembly Diagram. Join the pieces into horizontal rows, and then join rows to complete the block (Block Diagram). Made 6 red blocks, 4 pink blocks, 5 blue blocks, 6 green blocks, 5 gold blocks, and 4 theme-print blocks.

Diagram 1

Diagram 2

Diagram 3

Block Assembly Diagram

Block Diagram

Assembling the Quilt

1. Referring to photo, arrange the blocks in the order in which they will appear in the quilt.

2. Join the blocks into 6 horizontal rows of 5 blocks each.

3. Join the rows together to complete the quilt top.

Borders

1. Measure the length of the quilt top, measuring through the middle rather than along the sides. Trim 2 green print inner border strips to this length. Stitch 1 of these to each side of the quilt.

2. Measure the width of the quilt top, measuring through the middle rather than along the sides. Trim 2 green print inner border strips to this length. Stitch 1 of these to the top and bottom of the quilt.

3. Measure the length of the quilt top, measuring through the middle rather than along the sides. Trim 2 theme print outer border strips to this length. Stitch 1 of these to each side of the quilt.

4. Measure the width of the quilt top, measuring through the middle rather than along the sides. Trim 2 theme print outer border strips to this length. Stitch 1 of these to the top and bottom of the quilt.

Quilting and Finishing

1. Mark the desired quilting design on the quilt top. The quilt shown has outline quilting inside the Bow Ties, in-the-ditch quilting along the inner border, and a curved design in the outer border.

2. Layer backing, batting, and quilt top. Baste.

3. Quilt as desired.

4. Referring to the general instructions on page 21, make 162" of bias binding and apply to the quilt.

Stellar Jays

Quilt: 23" x 33"
Finished Block Size: 5" square

Stellar Jays by Michelle Ashley, 1995, Lemon Grove, California.

Bold and bright, these Jays will liven up a wall in your den. The Stepping Stone blocks

that frame the birds are easy to make. Using diagonal corners, you can stitch the Jays in a jiffy.

Materials

½ yard white for background

¼ yard navy print for Stepping Stones and Jay beaks

¼ yard dark blue print for Jay crests, bodies, and tails

⅛ yard medium blue print for Jay breasts

Scrap of tan for Jay faces

⅛ yard green print for leaves

¼ yard blue-and-white print for inner border

½ yard navy-and-green print for outer border

1 yard fabric for backing

1 yard batting

¼ yard fabric for binding

Cutting

From the *white,* cut:

• 1 (3½" x 26") strip for the Stepping Stone blocks.

• 2 (1½" x 42") strips for the Stepping Stone blocks. Divide the strips into 2 (1½" x 26") pieces and 2 (1½" x 14") pieces. Cut 1 (1½" x 26") strip into 14 (1½") squares.

• 1 (3½" x 42") strip. Cut the strip into 23 (1½" x 3½") pieces for the Stepping Stone blocks.

• 1 (3½" x 42") strip. Cut the strip into 7 (3½" x 4½") pieces for Jay block background.

• 1 (2½" x 42") strip. Cut the strip into 7 (2½") squares and 14 (1½" x 2½") pieces for Jay block background.

From the *navy print,* cut:

• 5 (1½" x 42") strips. Divide 3 of the strips into:

  • 4 (1½" x 26") pieces for the Stepping Stone blocks.

  • 1 (1½" x 14") pieces for the Stepping Stone blocks.

  • 7 (1½") squares for the Jay beaks.

From the *dark blue print,* cut:

• 1 (3½" x 42") strip. Cut the strip into 7 (3½") squares for the Jay bodies.

• 1 (1½" x 42") strip. Cut the strip into 28 (1½") squares for the Jay crests and tails.

From the *medium blue print,* cut:

• 1 (1½" x 42") strip. Cut the strip into 7 (1½" x 3½") pieces for the Jay breasts.

From the *tan scrap,* cut:

• 7 (1½") squares for the Jay faces.

From the *green print,* cut:

• 1 (1½" x 42") strip. Cut the strip into 21 (1½") squares for the leaves.

From the *blue-and-white print,* cut:

• 3 (1½" x 42") strips for inner borders.

From the *navy-and-green print,* cut:

• 4 (3¼" x 42") strips for outer borders.

Assembling the Blocks
Stepping Stone Blocks

1. Sew strip sets as shown in Strip Set Diagrams:

• 1 of Strip Set A using 1½" x 26" pieces of navy and 3½" x 26" piece of white—navy/white/navy.

• 1 of Strip Set B using 1½" x 26" pieces—navy/white/navy.

• 1 of Strip Set C using 1½" x 14" pieces—white/navy/white.

Press all seam allowances toward the darker fabrics.

2. Referring to Cutting Diagrams, cut:

• 16 (1½"-wide) segments from Strip Set A.

• 16 (1½"-wide) segments from Strip Set B.

• 8 (1½"-wide) segments from Strip Set C.

3. Join the segments and the 1½" x 3½" pieces of white as shown in the Block 1 Assembly Diagrams. Make 8 blocks. ·····················➤

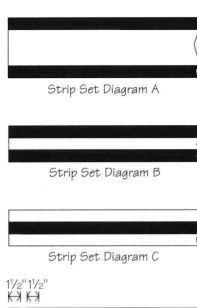

Strip Set Diagram A

Strip Set Diagram B

Strip Set Diagram C

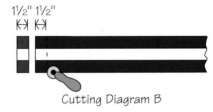

1½" 1½"

Cutting Diagram A

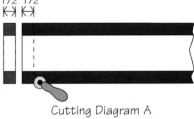

1½" 1½"

Cutting Diagram B

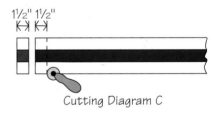

1½" 1½"

Cutting Diagram C

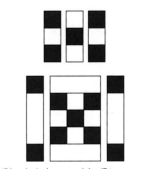

Block 1 Assembly Diagrams

Stellar Jay Block

Body and Tail

Referring to the general instructions on page 101, use the diagonal-corner method to sew the Stellar Jay blocks.

1. For the body section, sew a 3½" dark blue diagonal-corner square to the lower right corner of the 3½" x 4½" white rectangle (Diagram 1). Set this section aside.

2. For the tail section, sew a 1½" dark blue diagonal-corner square to the upper left corner of a 1½" x 3½" white rectangle as shown in Diagram 2.

3. Sew a 1½" green diagonal-corner square to the lower right corner of the same 1½" x 3½" white rectangle as in Step 2 (Diagram 3).

4. Sew the tail section to the body section as shown in Diagram 4.

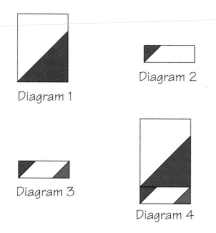

Diagram 1

Diagram 2

Diagram 3

Diagram 4

Head, Breast, and Beak

1. To make the leaf section, sew a 1½" green diagonal-corner square to the upper left corner of a 1½" x 2½" white rectangle (Diagram 5). Set this aside.

2. To make the head/breast section, sew a 1½" white diagonal-corner square to the lower right corner of the light blue rectangle as shown in Diagram 6.

3. Sew a tan diagonal-corner square to the upper right corner of the same light blue rectangle as shown in Diagram 7.

4. Sew a 1½" dark blue diagonal-corner square to the upper left corner of the same light blue rectangle, overlapping the tan as shown in Diagram 8.

5. Sew a 1½" dark blue square to the top of the same light blue rectangle as shown in Diagram 9. (*Note:* This is not a diagonal-corner piece.) Set this section aside.

6. To make the beak section, sew a green square to the lower right corner of a 1½" x 2½" white rectangle as shown in Diagram 10.

7. Sew a 1½" white square to the top of the same rectangle as in Step 6 as shown in Diagram 11. (*Note:* This is not a diagonal-corner piece.)

8. Sew the 1½" navy blue (beak) diagonal-corner square to the upper left corner of the 1½" white square as shown in Diagram 12.

9. Sew the head/breast section to the beak section as shown in Diagram 13.

10. Sew a 2½" white diagonal-corner square to the upper right corner of the head/breast/beak section. Sew the leaf section to the bottom of the head/breast/beak section (Diagram 14).

11. Join the 2 Jay halves as shown in the Block 2 Assembly Diagram. Make 7 blocks (Block 2 Diagram).

Assembling the Quilt Top

1. Referring to the photo, join the blocks alternately to each other in 5 horizontal rows of 3 blocks each as shown.

2. Join the rows together to complete the quilt top.

Diagram 5

Diagram 6

Diagram 7

Diagram 8

Diagram 9

Diagram 10

Diagram 11

Diagram 12

Diagram 13

Diagram 14

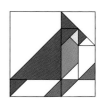

Block 2 Assembly Diagram

Block 2 Diagram

Borders

1. Measure the length of the quilt top, measuring through the middle rather than along the sides. Trim 2 blue-and-white inner border strips to this length. Stitch 1 of these to each side of the quilt.

2. Measure the width of the quilt top, measuring through the middle rather than along the sides. Trim 2 blue-and-white inner border strips to this length. Stitch 1 of these to the top and bottom of the quilt.

3. Measure the length of the quilt top, measuring through the middle rather than along the sides. Trim 2 navy-and-green print outer border strips to this length. Stitch 1 of these to each side of the quilt.

4. Measure the width of the quilt top, measuring through the middle rather than along the sides. Trim 2 navy-and-green print outer border strips to this length. Stitch 1 of these to the top and bottom of the quilt.

Quilting and Finishing

1. Mark the desired quilting designs on the quilt top. The quilt shown has outline quilting around the Jays, a wing shape in the Jay's body, a single line through the Stepping Stone blocks, and a curved design in the border.

2. Layer backing, batting, and quilt top. Baste.

3. Quilt as desired.

4. Referring to the general instructions on page 21, make 112" of bias binding and apply to the quilt.

Add the Unexpected to Your Quilt Back

This wild floral print had all of the colors I used on the front of the quilt, making it a perfect complement for the back. The plants almost have a "jungle feel" to them, so it is a little surprising when you turn up a quilt corner.

Liberty Bay, page 116.

Pictorial Pieced Quilts

One of the great delights of quilting is seeing familiar pictures forming out
of combinations of geometric shapes. The quilts in this chapter picture baskets,
houses, trees, and boats— all formed by combinations of simple shapes. In order to
cut some of those fabric shapes, you will need to make templates.

You can use freezer paper or plastic to
make your templates. If you are using
freezer paper (purchased in the grocery store in the area with the alu-
minum foil), simply trace the finished-
size pattern onto the dull side, cut out
the template, and press the shiny side
of the template onto the right side of
the fabric with a warm iron. Cut out
each piece ¼" from the freezer-paper
edge (Diagram 1). Each piece can be
reused several times before losing its
ability to adhere to the fabric.

To use plastic templates (poster-
board or sandpaper are sturdy replace-
ments), trace the pattern onto tracing
paper, cut out, and glue it to the template material; or trace it directly onto
the template plastic. (For machine
piecing, include seam allowance; for
hand piecing, trace the pattern finished
size.) Lay the template facedown on
the wrong side of the fabric or faceup
on the right side and trace (Diagram 2).

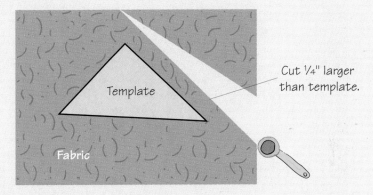

Cut ¼" larger
than template.

Diagram 1

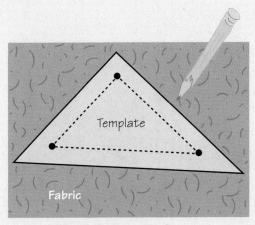

Diagram 2

Liberty Bay

Quilt: 45" x 47"
Finished Block Size: 6" square

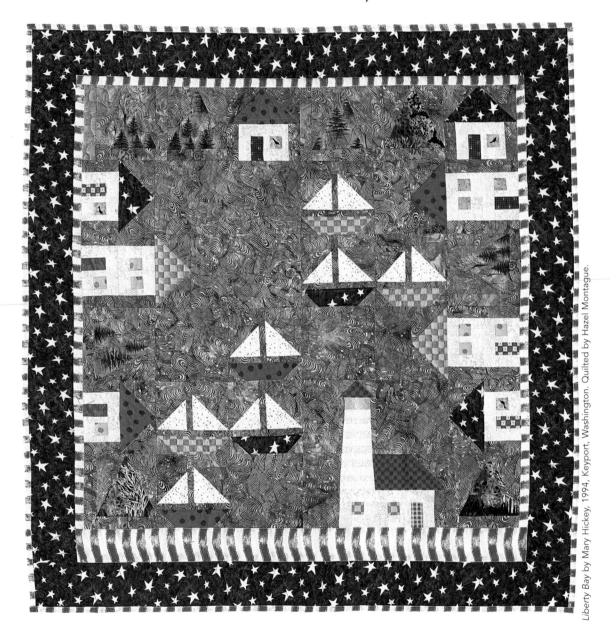

The long coastline of Washington state includes hundreds of little bays and coves.

This particular one, Liberty Bay, is my home. What fun to

make your own favorite bay, be it in Nantucket, New York, or Newport.

Materials

2½ yards blue print for background
½ yard beige print for houses
¼ yard white print for sails
¼ yard green print for trees
¼ yard gold prints for boat hulls, roofs, and windows
¼ yard red prints for boat hulls, roofs, and doors
¼ yard brown print for tree trunks
¼ yard red-and-white stripe for inner border
¾ yard navy star print for outer border
1½ yards backing fabric
1½ yards batting
⅝ yard fabric for binding

Sailboats
Cutting

From the *blue print*, cut:
• 2 (9") squares for A and B.
• 1 (2½" x 42") strip. Cut the strip into 14 (2½") squares for D.
• 4 (1" x 42") strips.
  • Cut 1 strip into 7 (1" x 3½") pieces for E.
  • Cut 1 strip into 7 (1" x 4") pieces for F.
• 1 (1½" x 42") strip. Cut the strip into 7 (1½" x 3") pieces for G.
• Cut 2 strips into 7 (1" x 6½") pieces for H.

From the *white print*, cut:
• 2 (9") squares for A and B.

From the *fabrics for the boat hulls*, cut:
• 7 (2½" x 6½") pieces for C. In the quilt shown, I used 3 gold, 2 red, and 2 navy boat hulls.

Assembling the Sailboat Blocks

1. Referring to the general instructions for making half-square triangles on pages 55–56, use the 9" squares of blue and white to make 7 (3") half-square triangle units (A) as follows:
• Cut the bias strips 3".
• Cut the segments 3".
• Cut the squares 3".
2. Referring to the general instructions

for making half-square triangles on pages 55–56, use the 9" squares of blue and white to make 7 (3½") half-square triangle units (B) as follows:
• Cut the bias strips 3½".
• Cut the segments 3½".
• Cut the squares 3½".
3. Referring to the general instructions for making diagonal corners on page 101, use the 2½" blue background squares (D) and the boat hull pieces (C) to make 7 boat hulls.
4. Arrange the pieces for each block as shown in the *Sailboat Block Assembly Diagram.* Join the pieces as shown to make 7 sailboat blocks.

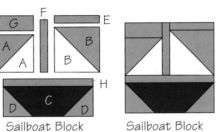

Sailboat Block
Assembly Diagram

Sailboat Block
Diagram

Houses (short and tall)
Cutting

From the *blue print*, cut:
• 1 (1½" x 42") strip. Cut the strip into 10 (1½" x 3½") pieces for I.
• 1 (1½" x 42") strip. Cut the strip into 6 (1½" x 6½") pieces for K.
• 1 (3⅞" x 42") strip. Cut the strip into 8 (3⅞") squares. Cut the squares in half diagonally to make 16 triangles for B.
• 3 (3½" x 6½") pieces for J.

From the *beige print*, cut:
• 3 (1½" x 20") strips. Cut these strips into:
  • 11 (1½" x 4½") pieces for H.
  • 11 (1½" x 2½") pieces for E.
  • 14 (1½") squares for D.
• 2 (1" x 42") strips. Cut each of the strips into 22 (1" x 2½") pieces for G.

From the *red, gold, and navy prints*, cut:
• 4 (6⅞") squares. Cut the squares in half diagonally to make As.

From the *red prints*, cut:
• 8 (1½" x 2½") pieces for F.

From the *gold print*, cut:
• 14 (1½") squares for C.

Assembling the Blocks

1. Referring to the House Block Assembly Diagrams, join 1 B to each side of A.
2. Join Cs and Ds in pairs.
3. Arrange the pieces for the house blocks as shown in the House Block Assembly Diagrams. Join the pieces as shown to make 5 short houses and 3 tall houses. ···············➤

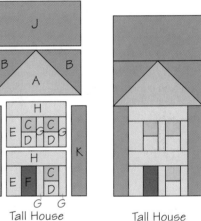

Tall House
Assembly Diagram

Tall House
Diagram

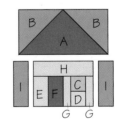

Short House
Assembly Diagram

Short House
Diagram

Trees
Cutting

From the *blue print*, cut:
- 3 (1½" x 42") strips.
  - Cut 2 of the strips into 8 (1½" x 6½") pieces for E.
  - Cut 1 of the strips into 16 (1½" x 2½") pieces for D.
- 8 (6¼") squares. Fold the squares in half from side to side. Cut the folded square diagonally from fold to corner to form the triangles for B (Diagram 1).

From the *green print*, cut:
- Cut 4 (5⅞") squares. Fold the squares in half from side to side. Cut the folded square diagonally from the fold to the corner as shown in Diagram 2 to form A.

From the *brown print*, cut:
- 8 (1½") squares for C.

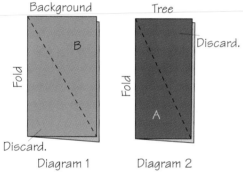

Diagram 1   Diagram 2

Assembling the Blocks

1. Referring to the Tree Block Assembly Diagram, join 1 B to each side of A.

2. Join 1 D to each side of C as shown.

3. Arrange the pieces for each block as shown in the Tree Assembly Diagram. Join pieces as shown to make 8 tree blocks.

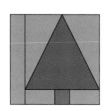

Tree Assembly Diagram   Tree Block Diagram

Lighthouse
Cutting

Make templates from patterns on page 120.

From the *blue print*, cut:
- 1 (3½" x 12½") piece for R.
- 1 (6½") square for Q.
- 2 (2") squares for G.
- 1 (3½") square for P.
- 1 (1½" x 3½") piece for N.
- 1 piece from Template C for the left side of the tower.
- 1 piece from Template D for the right side of the tower.

From the *red print*, cut:
- 1 (2" x 3½") piece for F.
- 1 (3½" x 6½") piece for O.
- 1 (1½" x 2½") piece for L.
- 1 piece from Template E for the part of the house roof next to the tower.

From the *yellow print*, cut:
- 2 (1½") squares for I.
- 1 piece from Template A for the light.

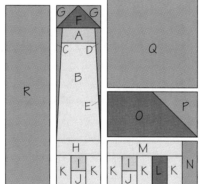

Lighthouse Assembly Diagram

From the *beige print*, cut:
- 1 (1½" x 42") strip. Cut the strip into:
  - 5 (1½" x 2½") pieces for K.
  - 1 (1½" x 3½") piece for H.
  - 1 (1½" x 5½") piece for M.
  - 2 (1½") squares for J.
- 1 piece from Template B for the tower.

Assembling the Block

1. Fold G squares in half diagonally and press a crease. Join Gs to F along the crease. Press and trim.

2. Fold P in half diagonally and crease. Using the diagonal-corners method, join P to the right side of O along the crease. Press and trim.

3. Sew A to the top of B. Sew D to the top of E. Join C to the left and D/E to the right of A/B. Join roof unit to top.

4. Arrange the pieces as shown in the Lighthouse Block Assembly Diagram. Join pieces to complete block.

Lighthouse Block Diagram

Repeat a Theme on the Back of Your Quilt

Sometimes I repeat elements on the back of my quilts. I like this terrific lighthouse print because it reflects the single pieced lighthouse on the front.

Setting Pieces and Borders

From the *blue print,* cut:
- 6 (6½") squares.

From the *red-and-white stripe,* cut:
- 3 (1¼" x 42") strips for top and side inner borders.
- 1 (3¼" x 42") strip for bottom inner border.

From the *navy star print,* cut:
- 5 (4¼" x 42") strips for outer borders.

Assembling the Quilt

1. Join the blocks into horizontal rows as shown in the *Quilt Top Assembly Diagram.*

2. Join the rows together to complete the quilt top.

Borders

1. Measure the length of the quilt top, measuring through the middle rather than along the sides. Trim 2 red-and-white stripe inner border strips to this length. Stitch 1 of these to each side of the quilt.

2. Measure the width of the quilt top, measuring through the middle rather than along the sides. Trim the 1¼" and the 3¼" inner border strips to this length. Stitch the narrow strip to the top of the quilt and the wide strip to the bottom of the quilt.

3. Measure the length of the quilt top, measuring through the middle rather than along the sides. Trim 2 navy star print outer border strips to this length.

Stitch 1 of these to each side of the quilt.

4. Measure the width of the quilt top, measuring through the middle rather than along the sides. Piece 2 navy star print outer border strips to this length. Stitch 1 of these to the top and bottom of the quilt.

Quilting and Finishing

1. Mark the desired quilting designs on the quilt top. The quilt shown has outline quilting around all the shapes.

2. Layer backing, batting, and quilt top. Baste.

3. Quilt as desired.

4. Referring to the general instructions on page 21, make 197" of bias binding and apply to the quilt. ························►

Quilt Top Assembly Diagram

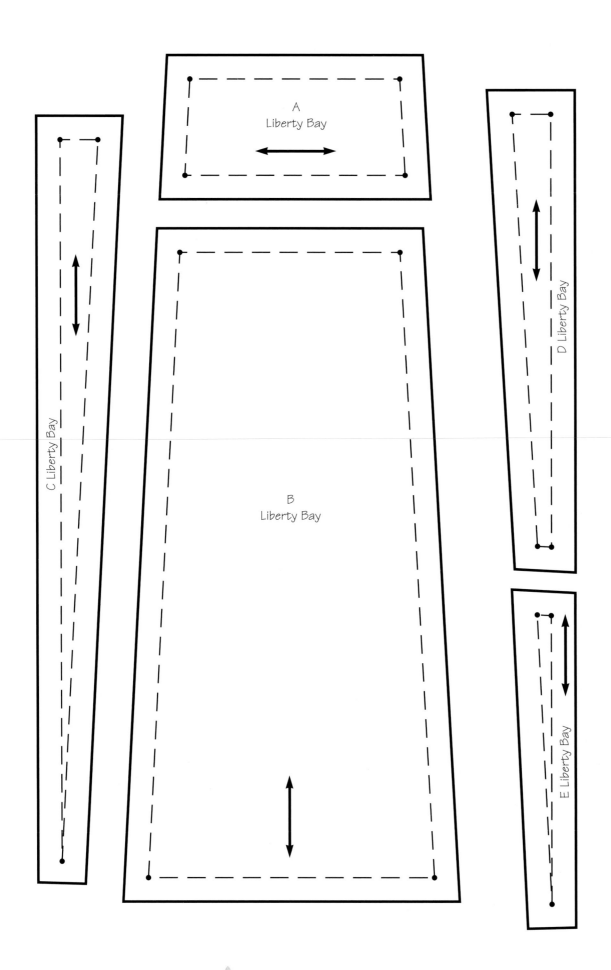

A
Liberty Bay

B
Liberty Bay

C Liberty Bay

D Liberty Bay

E Liberty Bay

Calypso Sailboats

Quilt: 37 ¾" x 47"
Finished Block Size: 6" square

Calypso Sailboats by Mary Hickey, 1995, Keyport, Washington. Quilted by the Ohio Amish.

These vibrant blocks recall the exhilaration that comes from sailing on a sunny

summer sea. With these easy blocks, the quilt is bound to become a treasure.

Materials

1½ yards aqua print for background (2 yards if fabric has a directional print)

1 yard white for sails and sashing squares

¼ yard or scrap lime green for boat hulls

¼ yard or scrap magenta for boat hulls

¼ yard or scrap green for boat hulls

¼ yard or scrap red for boat hulls

¼ yard or scrap blue for boat hulls

¼ yard or scrap gold for boat hulls

½ yard light turquoise for sashing strips

¼ yard magenta stripe for inner border

¾ yard dark turquoise print for outer border

1½ yards backing fabric

1½ yards batting

⅜ yard fabric for binding

Cutting

From the *aqua print*, cut:
• 3 (9" x 20") pieces for A and B.
• 3 (2½" x 42") strips. Cut the strips into 40 (2½") squares for D.
• 2 (1" x 42") strips. Cut the strips into 20 (1" x 3½") pieces for E.
• 2 (1" x 42") strips. Cut the strips into 20 (1" x 4") pieces for F. *Note:* If you are using a striped fabric, remember to cut so that all your pieces have the stripes going from side to side.
• 2 (1½" x 42") strips. Cut the strips into 20 (1½" x 3") pieces for G.
• 4 (1" x 42") strips. Cut the strips into 20 (1" x 6½") pieces for H.

From the *white*, cut:
• 3 (9" x 20") pieces for A and B.
• 2 (1¾" x 42") strips. Cut the strips into 30 (1¾") sashing squares.

From the *solid fabrics for boat hulls,* cut:
• 20 (2½" x 6½") pieces for C. In the quilt shown, I used 4 lime green, 2 magenta, 3 green, 4 red, 5 blue, and

2 gold boat hulls.

From the *light turquoise*, cut:
• 9 (1¾" x 42") strips. Cut the strips into 49 (1¾" x 6½") pieces for sashing strips.

From the *magenta stripe*, cut:
• 4 (1½" x 42") strips for the inner border.

From the *dark turquoise*, cut:
• 5 (4" x 42") strips for the outer border.

Assembling the Blocks

1. Referring to the general instructions for making half-square triangles on pages 55–56, use the 9" x 20" pieces of aqua and white to make 20 (3") half-square triangle units as follows. If you are using a striped fabric, remember to position your fabric so that the stripes will run from side to side.
• Cut the bias strips 3".
• Cut the segments 3".
• Cut the squares 3".

2. Referring to the general instructions for making half-square triangles on pages 55–56, use the 9" x 20" pieces of aqua and white to make 20 (3½") half-square triangle units as follows. If you are using a striped fabric, remember to position your fabric so that the stripes

will run from side to side.
• Cut the bias strips 3½".
• Cut the segments 3½".
• Cut the squares 3½".

3. Referring to the general instructions for diagonal corners on page 101, use the 2½" aqua squares (D) and the boat hull pieces (C) to stitch 20 boat hulls. If you are using a striped fabric, remember to place your fabric so that the stripes will run from side to side.

4. Arrange the pieces for each block as shown in the Block Assembly Diagram. Join the pieces to complete the block (Block Diagram). Make 20 blocks.

Assembling the Quilt

1. Join 4 light turquoise sashing strips with 1 white square between each piece and on each end of the strip as shown in Diagram 1. Make 6 sashing rows.

2. Join 4 blocks into a row with a sashing strip between the blocks and on each end of the row as shown in Diagram 2. Make 5 block rows.

3. Join the block rows with a sashing row between each row as shown in the Quilt Top Assembly Diagram. Sew a sashing row to the top and bottom of the quilt.

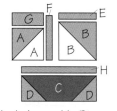

Block Assembly Diagram

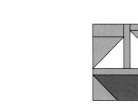

Block Diagram

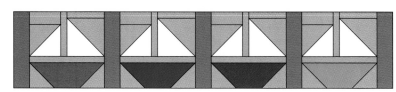

Diagram 1

Diagram 2

Borders

1. See general instructions on page 16 for tips on mitered border construction. Piece 2 side borders at least 50" long.
2. Stitch the borders to the quilt top, mitering the corners.

Quilting and Finishing

1. Mark the desired quilting designs on the quilt top. The quilt shown has outline quilting inside and outside the shapes of the sails and boat hulls, straight lines in the vertical sashing, a wave pattern in the horizontal sashing, straight lines in the inner border, and a wave pattern in the outer border.
2. Layer backing, batting, and quilt top. Baste.
3. Quilt as desired.
4. Referring to the general instructions on page 21, make 170" of bias binding and apply to the quilt.

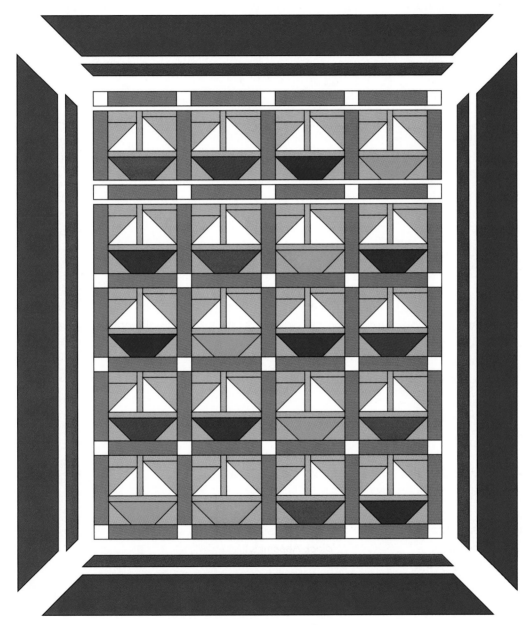

Quilt Top Assembly Diagram

Lace Baskets

Quilt: 29" x 36"
Finished Block Size: 5" square

A collection of doilies stitched into the seams creates pattern and dimension

on these easy baskets. Choose a variety of medium colors

to contrast with the lacy handwork; then add a festive floral border.

Materials

¾ yard white for background in blocks and setting blocks

¼ yard each or scraps of rose, blue, green and yellow for baskets

12 lace, tatted, cutwork, or crocheted doilies

¼ yard rose print for inner border

¾ yard floral print for setting triangles and outer border

1 yard fabric for backing

1 yard batting

⅜ yard fabric for binding

Cutting

From the *white,* cut:

• 6 (4⅞") squares. Cut the squares in half diagonally to make 12 triangles for the top half of the basket blocks.

• 6 (2⅞") squares. Cut the squares in half diagonally to make 12 triangles for the base of the basket blocks.

• 2 (1½" x 42") strips. Cut the strips into 24 (1½" x 3½") pieces for the sides of the basket blocks.

• 6 (5½") squares for setting blocks.

From the *scraps of rose, blue, green, and gold,* cut:

• 6 (4⅞") squares. Cut the squares in half diagonally to make 12 triangles for the baskets.

• 12 (1⅞") squares. Cut the squares in half diagonally to make 24 triangles for the basket bases.

• 12 (1¼" x 8") bias strips for the basket handles.

From the *rose print,* cut:

• 4 (1" x 42") strips for the inner border.

From the *floral print,* cut:

• 3 (8") squares. Cut the squares in quarters diagonally to make 12 side setting triangles (you will have 2 extra).

• 2 (4⅞") squares. Cut the squares in half diagonally to make 4 corner triangles.

• 4 (3½" x 42") strips for outer borders.

Assembling the Blocks

1. Referring to the general instructions on page 133 for bias-strip appliqué, appliqué the 1¼" x 8" bias strips to the large white background triangles for basket handles.

2. Arrange the pieces for each block as shown in the Block Assembly Diagram. Pin or baste the doilies in place. *Note:* It is not a good idea to cut your doilies in half, as they will come unravelled. Instead, press them in half and position them so that half covers the front of the basket and the other half falls behind the basket.

3. Make blocks as shown (Block Assembly Diagram). Make 12 blocks.

Assembling the Quilt

1. Join the blocks and setting pieces in diagonal rows as shown in the Quilt Top Assembly Diagram. Pin and carefully sew all match points.

2. Join the rows together to complete the quilt top.

Borders

1. See general instructions on page 16 for tips on mitered border construction.

2. Stitch the borders to the quilt top, mitering corners.

Quilting and Finishing

1. Mark the desired quilting designs on the quilt top. The quilt shown has outline quilting around the shapes in the Basket blocks, a flower in the setting blocks, and straight line and curved designs in the borders.

2. Layer backing, batting, and quilt top. Baste.

3. Quilt as desired.

4. Referring to the general instructions on page 21, make 134" of bias binding and apply to the quilt.

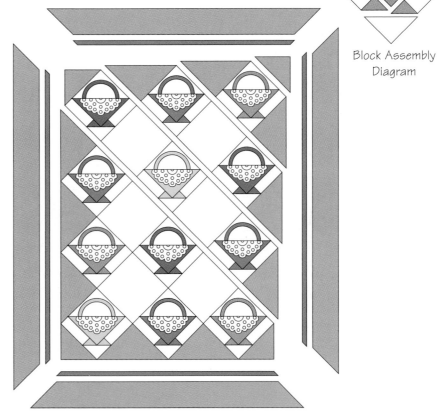

Block Assembly Diagram

Quilt Top Assembly Diagram

Spring Cottages

Quilt: 32½" x 32½"
Finished Block Size: 6" square

Spring Cottages by Mary Hickey, 1995, Keyport, Washington.

A profusion of rose vines border these dainty English cottages.

The house and tree pieces are large and easy to sew. If you have a collection of calicoes

on hand, this is the perfect opportunity to use them in a scrappy quilt.

Notice that I reversed the placement of the door and window in one house block.

Materials

1 yard or scraps white calicos for background

⅓ yard or scraps green prints for trees and roofs

½ yard or scraps pink prints for doors, windows, cottages, and sashing

¼ yard or scraps yellow prints for cottages and windows

⅓ yard or scraps dark pink prints for doors, tree trunks, and inner border

½ yard yellow floral print for outer borders

1 yard fabric for backing

1 yard batting

⅓ yard fabric for binding

Cutting

From the *white calicos,* cut:

- 4 (1½" x 42") strips. From these:
  - Cut 2 strips into 18 (1½" x 3½") pieces for I.
  - Cut 1 strip into 3 (1½" x 6½") pieces for N.
  - Cut 1 strip into 6 (1½" x 2½") pieces for M.
- 1 (3⅞" x 42") strip. Cut the strip into 9 (3⅞") squares. Cut the squares in half diagonally to make 18 triangles for B.
- 3 (6¼") squares. Fold the squares in half from side to side. Cut the folded square diagonally from fold to corner to form triangles for K (Diagram 1).

From the *light yellow and pink prints,* cut:

- 1 (1½" x 20") strip from each color (6 yellows and 3 pinks). Cut each strip as follows for the fronts of the houses:
  - 1½" x 4½" for H.
  - 1½" x 2½" for E.
  - 1½" square for D.
  - 1" x 6" strip. Cut the strip into 2 (1" x 2½") pieces for G.

From the *pink prints,* cut:

- 1 (1½" x 20") strip. Cut the strip into 9 (1½") squares for C.

- 4 (2" x 42") strips for the horizontal sashing.

From the *green prints,* cut:

- 5 (5⅛") squares. Cut each square in half diagonally to make A (you will have 1 extra).
- 3 (5⅞") squares. Fold the squares in half from side to side. Cut the folded squares diagonally from the fold to the corner to form J (Diagram 2).

From *dark pink print,* cut:

- 4 (1½") squares for L.
- 1 (1½" x 42") strip. Cut the strip into 9 (1½" x 2½") pieces for F.
- 4 (1" x 42") strips for inner borders.

From the *yellow floral print,* cut:

- 4 (4" x 42") strips for outer borders.

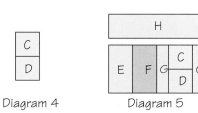

Diagram 1   Diagram 2

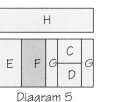

Diagram 4   Diagram 5

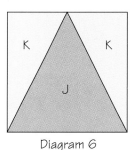

Diagram 6

Diagram 7

Assembling the Blocks
Houses

1. Join 1 B to each side of A to make roof unit (Diagram 3).

2. Join Cs and Ds in pairs (Diagram 4).

3. Join the remaining house pieces as shown in Diagram 5. Add I pieces to each side of the house unit.

4. Join this unit to the roof unit as shown in *Block 1 Assembly Diagram.* Make 9 blocks.

Trees

1. Join 1 K to each side of J to make tree top unit (Diagram 6).

2. Join 1 M to each side of L to make trunk unit (Diagram 7).

3. Arrange the pieces for each block as shown in *Block 2 Assembly Diagram.* Make 3 blocks.

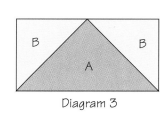

Diagram 3

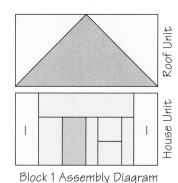

Block 1 Assembly Diagram

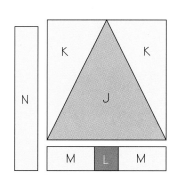

Block 2 Assembly Diagram

Assembling the Quilt

1. Join the blocks in 3 horizontal rows of 4 blocks each as shown in the *Quilt Top Assembly Diagram*.

2. Place a sashing strip between each row and at the top and bottom.

3. Join the sashing and rows to complete the quilt top.

Borders

1. Measure the length of the quilt top, measuring through the middle rather than along the sides. Trim 2 dark pink print inner border strips to this length. Stitch 1 of these to each side of the quilt.

2. Measure the width of the quilt top, measuring through the middle rather than along the sides. Trim 2 dark pink inner border strips to this length. Stitch 1 of these to the top and bottom of the quilt.

3. Measure the length of the quilt top, measuring through the middle rather than along the sides. Trim 2 floral print outer border strips to this length. Stitch 1 of these to each side of the quilt.

4. Measure the width of the quilt top, measuring through the middle rather than along the sides. Trim 2 floral print outer border strips to this length. Stitch 1 of these to the top and bottom of the quilt.

Quilting and Finishing

1. Mark the desired quilting designs on the quilt top. The quilt shown has outline quilting ½" inside the roofs and trees, and in-the-ditch quilting around the sides, windows, doors, houses, and trees. Three rows of echo quilting surround each house and tree. A curved design appears in the sashing and a cable in the outer border.

2. Layer backing, batting, and quilt top. Baste.

3. Quilt as desired.

4. Referring to the general instructions on page 21, make 130" of bias binding and apply to the quilt.

Quilt Top Asembly Diagram

Christmas Cabins

Quilt: 24½" x 24½"
Finished Block Size: 6" square

Christmas Cabins by Joan Hanson, 1994, Seattle, Washington.

Cozy cabins nestled in the trees proclaim the

coming of winter holidays. The houses and trees are easy to make

and are a loving symbol of the warmth of home and family.

Materials

¾ yard black print for background

½ yard or scraps red prints for houses and outer border (you will need at least 5 reds)

¼ yard or scraps green print for trees, front doors, and corners of borders (you will need 5 greens)

⅛ yard or scrap yellow print for windows

⅛ yard or scrap brown print for tree trunks

1 yard fabric for backing

1 yard batting

¼ yard fabric for binding

Note: The blocks for *Christmas Cabins* are the same as those used in *Spring Cottages.* Refer to the diagrams on page 127 and below. Reverse the positions of C/D and F in three blocks.

Cutting

From the *black print,* cut:
- 5 (1½" x 42") strips. From these:
  - Cut 1 strip into 10 (1½" x 3½") pieces for I.
  - Cut 1 strip into 5 (1½" x 6½") pieces for N.
  - Cut 1 strip into 8 (1½" x 2½") pieces for M.
  - Cut 2 of the strips into 4 (1½" x 20") pieces for inner borders.
- 1 (3⅞" x 20") strip. Cut the strip into 5 (3⅞") squares. Cut the squares in half diagonally to make 10 triangles for B.
- 4 (6¼") squares. Fold the squares in half from side to side. Cut the folded square diagonally from fold to corner to form K (Diagram 1).

From the *red prints,* cut:
- 1 (1½" x 20") strip from 5 reds. Cut each strip into the following pieces for the front of the houses:
  - 1½ x 4½" for H.
  - 1½ x 2½ for E.
  - 1½" square for D.

- 1 (1" x 6") strip. Cut each the strip into 2 (1" x 2½") pieces for G.
- 3 (5⅛") squares. Cut each square in half diagonally to make A (you will have 1 extra).
- 4 (2½" x 20") strips for the outer border.

From the *green scraps,* cut:
- Cut 1 (1½" x 20") strip. Cut the strip into 5 (1½" x 2½") pieces for F.
- Cut 4 (5⅞") squares. Fold the squares in half from side to side. Cut the folded squares diagonally from fold to corner to form J (Diagram 2).
- Cut 2 (2½") squares for the border corners.

From the *yellow print,* cut:
- 5 (1½") squares for C.

From the *brown print,* cut:
- 4 (1½") squares for L.

Assembling the Blocks

Houses

1. Join 1 B to each side of A to make roof unit (Diagram 3).

2. Join Cs to Ds in pairs (Diagram 4).

3. Join the remaining house pieces as shown in Diagram 5. Add I pieces to each side of the house unit.

4. Join this unit to the roof unit as shown in the Block 1 Assembly Diagram. Make 5 blocks.

Trees

1. Join 1 K to each side of J to make tree top unit (Diagram 6).

2. Join 1 M to each side of L to make trunk unit (Diagram 7).

3. Arrange the pieces for each block as shown in Block 2 Assembly Diagram. Make 4 blocks.

Assembling the Quilt

1. Make 2 rows by joining a house block to each side of 1 tree block.

2. Make 1 row by joining a tree block to each side of 1 house block.

3. Join the rows together.

Borders

1. Measure the length of the quilt top, measuring through the middle rather than along the sides. Trim 2 black print inner border strips to this length. Stitch 1 of these to each side of the quilt.

2. Measure the width of the quilt top, measuring through the middle rather than along the sides. Trim 2 black print inner border strips to this length. Stitch 1 of these to the top and bottom of the quilt.

3. Measure the length of the quilt top, measuring through the middle rather than along the sides. Trim 4 red print outer border strips to this length. Stitch 2 of these to the sides of the quilt.

4. Join the green print squares to the ends of the 2 remaining strips. Stitch these to the top and bottom of the quilt.

Quilting and Finishing

1. Mark the desired quilting designs on the quilt top. The quilt shown has outline quilting ½" inside the roofs, trees, and borders, and in-the-ditch quilting around the sides, windows, doors, houses, and trees.

2. Layer backing, batting, and quilt top. Baste.

3. Quilt as desired.

4. Referring to the general instructions on page 21, make 98" of bias binding and apply to the quilt.

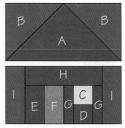

Block 1 Assembly Diagram

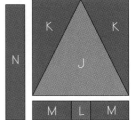

Block 2 Assembly Diagram

Garden Trellis

Quilt: 33" x 33"
Finished Block Size: 5¾" square

When these truly simple X blocks come together, they form an intricate trellis design.

Careful color placement and easy sewing techniques are all you need

to complete this little quilt.

Materials

¾ yard turquoise floral print for background and outer border
½ yard light aqua print for trellis and inner border
½ yard dark aqua print for trellis and middle border
½ yard light pink print for trellis
½ yard dark pink print for trellis
1 yard fabric for backing
1 yard batting
⅜ yard fabric for binding

Cutting

From the *turquoise floral print*, cut:
• 2 (4" x 42") strips. Cut the strips into 16 (4") squares. Cut the squares in quarters diagonally to make 64 triangles for the background.
• 4 (3¼" x 42") strips for outer borders.

From the *light aqua print*, cut:
• 4 (1½" x 42") strips for the trellis.
• 4 (1" x 42") strips for inner borders.

From the *dark aqua print*, cut:
• 4 (1½" x 42") strips for the trellis.
• 4 (1½" x 42") strips for the middle border.

From the *light pink print*, cut:
• 4 (1½" x 42") strips for the trellis.
• 1 (2¼" x 42") strip. Cut the strip into 8 (2¼") squares. Cut the squares in half diagonally to make 16 triangles.

From the *dark pink print*, cut:
• 4 (1½" x 42") strips for the trellis.
• 1 (2¼" x 42") strip. Cut the strip into 8 (2¼") squares. Cut the squares in half diagonally to make 16 triangles.

Assembling the Blocks

1. Join the light aqua print and dark aqua print strips together in lengthwise pairs. Press the seams open.
2. Cut across the strips at 6⅝" intervals, creating 16 (2½" x 6⅝") segments (Diagram 1).

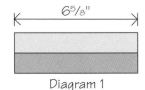

Diagram 1

3. Join the light pink print and dark pink strips together in lengthwise pairs. Press the seams open.
4. Fold the sewn pairs in half. With the strips folded, cut across them at 3⅝" intervals, creating 16 pairs of 2½" x 3⅝" segments (Diagram 2).
5. Keeping pink segments layered in pairs, place the corner of a ruler at the edge of the segments and the 45°-angle line on the seam. Trim 1 end of the segments to a right angle as shown in Diagram 3.
6. Arrange the pieces for each block as shown in the Block Assembly Diagram. Join the pieces as shown to complete the block (Block Diagram). Make 16 blocks.

Assembling the Quilt

1. Join the blocks in 4 horizontal rows of 4 blocks each as shown in the Quilt Top Assembly Diagram. Pin and carefully sew all match points.
2. Join the rows together to complete the quilt top.

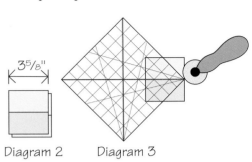

Diagram 2   Diagram 3

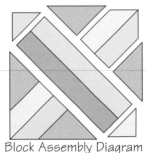

Block Assembly Diagram

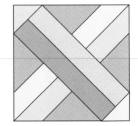

Block Diagram

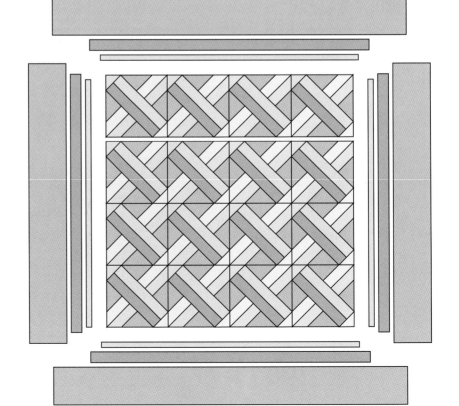

Quilt Top Assembly Diagram

Borders

1. Measure the length of the quilt top, measuring through the middle rather than along the sides. Trim 2 light aqua print inner border strips to this length. Stitch 1 of these to each side of the quilt.

2. Measure the width of the quilt top, measuring through the middle rather than along the sides. Trim 2 light aqua print inner border strips to this length. Stitch 1 of these to the top and bottom of the quilt.

3. Measure the length of the quilt top, measuring through the middle rather than along the sides. Trim 2 dark aqua print middle border strips to this length. Stitch 1 of these to each side of the quilt.

4. Measure the width of the quilt top, measuring through the middle rather than along the sides. Trim 2 dark aqua print middle border strips to this length. Stitch 1 of these to the top and bottom of the quilt.

5. Measure the length of the quilt top, measuring through the middle rather than along the sides. Trim 2 floral print outer border strips to this length. Stitch 1 of these to each side of the quilt.

6. Measure the width of the quilt top, measuring through the middle rather than along the sides. Trim 2 floral print outer strips to this length. Stitch 1 of these to the top and bottom of the quilt.

Quilting and Finishing

1. Mark the desired quilting designs on the quilt top. The quilt shown has outline quilting around the shapes in the trellis and a cable design in the border.

2. Layer backing, batting, and quilt top. Baste.

3. Quilt as desired.

4. Referring to the general instructions on page 21, make 132" of bias binding and apply to the quilt.

Handy Tips for Working With Bias Strip Appliqué

Bias marking bars, inexpensive tools that you can purchase at quilt shops, can help you make perfect bias appliqué strips. These special flat instruments allow you to hide the exposed seam without having to make a fabric tube that must be turned right side out.

1. Begin with a square cut from your fabric of choice. The square can be almost any size, depending upon how long you want your strips to be. The longest strip will be cut along the center diagonal. Aligning the 45° markings on your acrylic ruler with the bottom of your fabric, make a diagonal cut across the square from corner to corner. Continue making bias cuts in the desired width (*photo A*).

Since you have cut along the bias, the strips will be very stretchy—handle with care! Remember that strips can be joined with a diagonal seam to make a longer strip, if needed.

2. *With wrong sides facing,* fold the strip in half and stitch the bias strip into a tube using a scant ¼" seam allowance.

3. Insert the bias bar inside the fabric tube (*photo B*). Twist the tube so that the seam falls on the flat side.

4. Press the tube flat, with the bias bar still inside (*photo C*). The seam allowance will flatten, and you will have crisp edges. CAUTION: Many bias bars are metal, and they get very hot when pressed! Be careful as you remove the fabric from the bar.

5. Since you have cut your fabric on the bias, it will curve any way you position it (*photo D*). The seam allowance is neatly hidden, and appliquéing a thin strip is no longer a challenge.

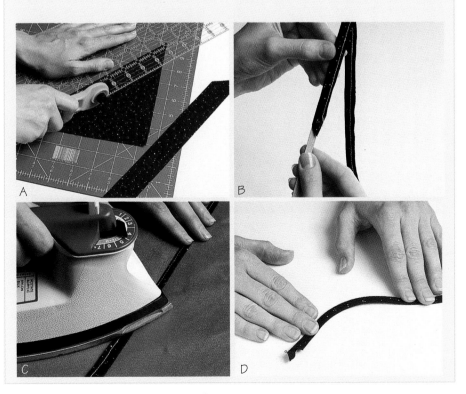

May Baskets

Quilt: 30" x 30"
Finished Block Size: 5" square

May Baskets by Mary Hickey, 1994, Keyport, Washington. Quilted by Hazel Montague.

Petite baskets in dainty colors perch among delicate blue squares.

The basket colors coordinate with the border stripe to complete this elegant little quilt.

Materials

½ yard white for block backgrounds
¼ yard or scraps of blue prints for baskets
¼ yard or scraps of pink prints for large triangle in baskets
½ yard light blue print for setting pieces
1 yard striped fabric for border
1 yard fabric for backing
1 yard batting
¼ yard fabric for binding

Cutting

From the *white*, cut:
• 2 (6") squares.
• 5 (4⅞") squares. Cut the squares in half diagonally to make 10 triangles.
• 5 (2⅞") squares. Cut the squares in half diagonally to make 10 triangles.
• 2 (1½ x 42") strips. Cut the strips into:
   • 18 (1½" x 3½") pieces.
   • 9 (1½") squares.

From the *blue prints*, cut:
• 2 (6") squares for the baskets.
• 9 (2⅜") squares. Cut the squares in quarters diagonally to make 4 triangles from each square.
• 9 (1¼" x 8") bias strips for the basket handles.

From the *pink prints*, cut:
• 3 (4") squares. Cut the squares in quarters diagonally to make 4 triangles from each square for the large basket triangles.

From the *light blue print*, cut:
• 4 (5½") setting squares.
• 2 (8") squares. Cut the squares in quarters diagonally to make the side setting triangles.
• 2 (4⅞") squares. Cut the squares in half diagonally to make the corner triangles.

From the *striped fabric*, cut:
• 4 (4¾" x 42") lengthwise strips for the outer border.

Assembling the Blocks

1. Referring to the general instructions for making half-square triangles on pages 55–56, use the 6" squares of white and blue print to make 36 (1½") half-square triangle units as follows:
• Cut the bias strips 1¾".
• Cut the segments 1½".
• Cut the squares 1½".
2. Referring to the general instructions for bias-strip appliqué on page 133, use the 1¼" x 8" bias strips of blue to appliqué the basket handles to the large white background triangles (Diagram 1).
3. Arrange the matching pieces for each basket section as shown in Diagram 2. Join into 1 unit.
4. Arrange the pieces for each block as shown in the Block Assembly Diagram. Join the pieces to complete the block. Make 9 blocks.

Assembling the Quilt

1. Join the blocks in diagonal rows as shown in the Quilt Top Assembly Diagram. Pin and carefully sew all match points.

2. Join the rows together to complete the quilt top.

Borders

1. See general instructions on page 16 for tips on mitered border construction.
2. Stitch the borders to the quilt top, mitering the corners.

Quilting and Finishing

1. Mark the desired quilting designs on the quilt top. The quilt shown has outline quilting around the shapes in the Basket blocks, a wreath in the setting blocks, and straight line and curved designs in the borders.
2. Layer backing, batting, and quilt top. Baste.
3. Quilt as desired.
4. Referring to the general instructions on page 21, make 120" of bias binding and apply to the quilt.

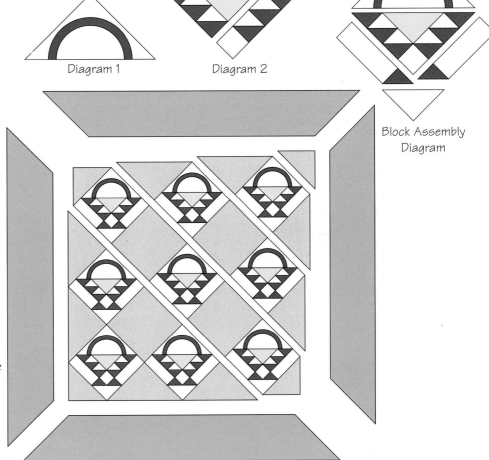

Diagram 1   Diagram 2

Block Assembly Diagram

Quilt Top Assembly Diagram

Cosmic Star, page 140.

Quilts Made with Half Rectangles

Long, thin triangles can be hard to sew because you can't see where to match up the points.

Try to think of them the same way you think of half-square triangles. Those are a snap

to make using bias-cut strips. You can make long triangles using the same

techniques. The only differences are that you fold the fabric and use a slightly different angle.

A BiRangle™, a rectangular ruler with a diagonal line, makes cutting long triangles easy and accurate. If you do not have or cannot obtain this ruler, the instructions on page 139 explain how to adapt your cutting ruler to do this specialized job.

Half-rectangle Triangles

1. Cut a piece of two printed fabrics. (The size you need for each quilt will be specified in the instructions.)

2. Stack both fabrics right side up. Fold the layered fabrics in half lengthwise. Trim off the fold.

3. With the fabrics layered, place a rectangular ruler with the diagonal line on the left cut edge of the fabrics and make an angled cut (Diagram 1).

4. Cut strips parallel to the angled cut (Diagram 2).

5. Sort the strips into two stacks—the up-facing ones in one set and the down-facing ones in the other.

6. Arrange the strips in each stack to make two strip sets, alternating the colors (Diagram 3).

7. Sew the strips into two strip sets, offsetting the tops of the strips ¼" (Diagram 4). Press the seams of one strip set toward the darker color and the second strip set toward the lighter color.

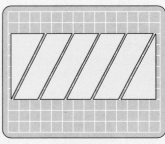

Diagram 1

Diagram 2

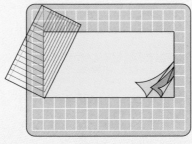

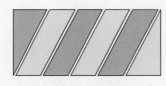

Diagram 3

Diagram 4

8. Since this is an odd angle, one of your strip sets will have the angle sloping down to the right and one will have the angle sloping down to the left. Start with the strip set that slopes down to the right. Position a small ruler with the diagonal line on one of the inner seams. Using the small ruler as a guide, place a large rectangular ruler to the left as a straight-edge cutting guide (Diagram 5). Remove the smaller ruler and trim the edge of the strip set to a perfect angle with the seams.

9. Cut a segment the width indicated in the instructions.

10. Place a rectangular ruler with the edge of the ruler on the cut edge of the fabric and the diagonal line on the seam line, as shown in Diagram 6. Cut on the right side of the ruler. Notice that the diagonal line should not come through the corner of the rectangle.

11. Position the ruler in the same manner on each seam line and trim (Diagram 7).

12. Turn the cut pieces around so that the untrimmed edge is on the right, reposition the ruler with the edge of the ruler on the edge of the fabric and the diagonal line on the seam, and cut (Diagram 8).

13. Before you cut another segment from the strip unit, be certain to place the ruler with the diagonal line on the seam line and trim the edge to a perfect 38° angle with the seam line (Diagram 9).

14. Check to be sure the sewn rectangle is exactly ½" larger than the finished size.

15. *Important:* Cut the strip set that slopes down to the left from the wrong side of the fabrics; in other words, with the fabrics facing down (Diagram 10).

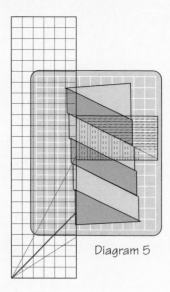

Diagram 5

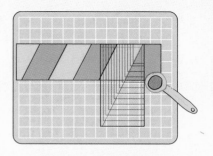

Diagram 6

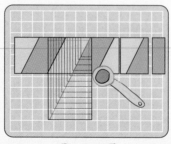

Diagram 7

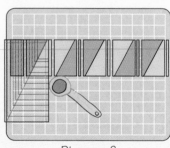

Diagram 8

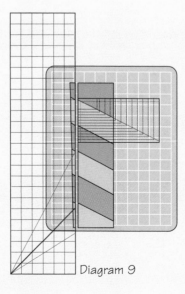

Diagram 9

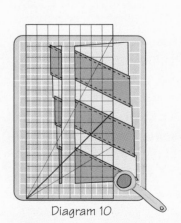

Diagram 10

Preparing Your 6" x 24" Ruler

If you do not have or cannot obtain a BiRangle™ ruler, follow these instructions for adapting your 6" x 24" ruler.

1. Referring to *Marking Diagram*, place the ruler horizontally on a table with the wrong side up (numbers will be reversed).

2. Using a fine-point permanent marker, mark ¼" seam lines parallel to two perpendicular edges as shown in red.

3. To make the half-rectangle line, draw a line from the top right ⅛" mark down to the 3⅛" mark on the bottom edge. (Marking points are shown in blue circles for easier reference.)

Tip: If you make a mistake with your permanent marker, rubber-cement thinner applied with a tissue will remove the marks.

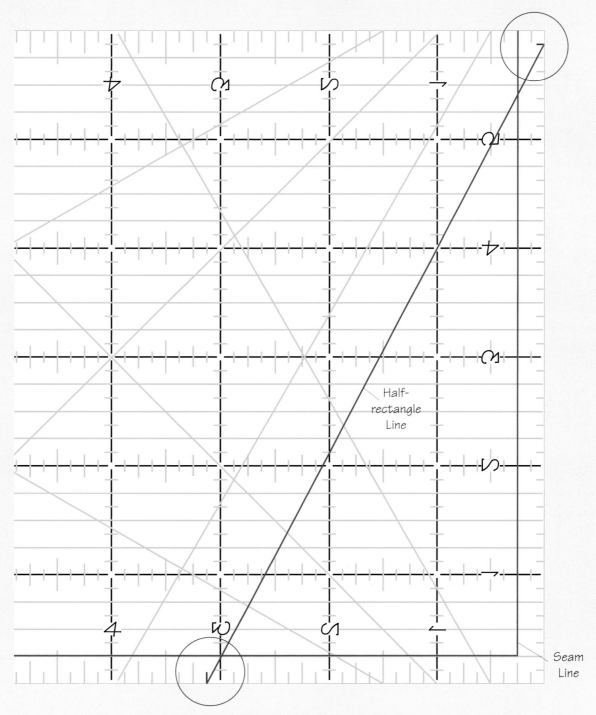

Half-rectangle Line

Seam Line

Marking Diagram

Cosmic Star

Quilt: 42½" x 42½"
Finished Block Size: 10½" square

Cosmic Star by Mary Hickey, 1994, Keyport, Washington. Quilted by Gretchen Engle.

The bias strip-piecing technique makes sewing the star points in this
quilt a breeze. The illusion of curves occurs when the tips
of the star triangles touch the tips of the large Snowball triangles.

Materials

2 yards blue print for background and outer border

½ yard light yellow print for star triangles and squares

⅛ yard gold print for four-patch squares

¼ yard rust for center squares and inner border

½ yard yellow stripe for wide triangles and middle border

1¼ yards fabric for backing

1¼ yards batting

⅜ yard fabric for binding

Cutting

From the *blue print*, cut:
- 6 (2" x 42") strips for rectangles, four-patches, and nine-patches. Cut 2 of the strips into 16 (2" x 3½") pieces.
- 1 (9" x 42") piece for half-rectangle triangles.
- 5 (11") squares for Snowball blocks.
- 4 (3¼" x 42") strips for outer border.

From the *light yellow print*, cut:
- 1 (9" x 42") piece for half-rectangle triangles.
- 1 (2" x 42") strip. Cut the strip in half to create 2 (2" x 21") half-strips for nine-patches.

From the *gold print*, cut:
- 2 (2" x 42") strips for four-patches.

From the *rust*, cut:
- 1 (2" x 20") strip. Cut the strip into 4 (2") squares for star centers.
- 1 (2" x 21") strip for nine-patches.
- 4 (1" x 42") strips for inner border.

From the *yellow stripe*, cut:
- 2 (3½"-wide) strips. Cut the strips into 20 (3½") squares for Snowball corners.
- 4 (2" x 42") strips for middle border.

Assembling the Blocks
Star Blocks

1. Referring to the general instructions for making half-rectangle triangles on pages 137–138, use the 9" x 42" pieces of blue and light yellow to make 32 half-rectangle triangles (16 with yellow on the left and 16 with yellow on the right) as follows:
- Cut the bias strips 2½".
- Cut the segments 3½".
- Cut the rectangles 2" x 3½".

2. Join the star points with a 2" x 3½" blue rectangle in the middle of each pair. Be careful to stitch the background color to the background color as shown in Diagram 1. Make 16 units.

3. Sew 1 (2" x 42") gold strip to 1 blue strip to make a strip set, as shown in Diagram 2. Repeat to make a second strip set.

4. Cut across the strip sets at 2" intervals to make 32 segments (Diagram 3).

5. Stitch the segments together as shown in Diagram 4 to make 16 four-patches.

6. Cut 2 (2" x 42") blue strips in half.

7. Stitch 2 strip sets from the half-strips as follows: light yellow/blue/light yellow (Diagram 5) and blue/rust/blue (Diagram 6).

8. Cut across the strip sets at 2" intervals to make 8 yellow/blue/yellow segments and 4 blue/rust/blue segments.

9. Stitch the segments together as shown in Diagram 7 to make 4 nine-patches.

10. Referring to Block 1 Assembly Diagram, arrange the pieces as shown.

11. Join the pieces to make 4 blocks as shown in the Block 1 Diagram.

Diagram 1

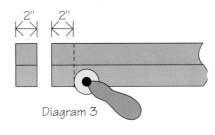

Diagram 2

Diagram 3

Diagram 4

Diagram 5

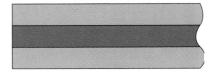

Diagram 6

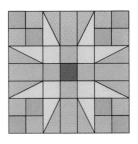

Diagram 7

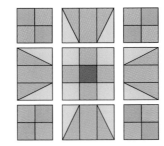

Block 1 Assembly Diagram

Block 1 Diagram

Snowball Blocks

1. Fold the 3½" yellow stripe squares in half diagonally and press a crease (Diagram 8).

2. With right sides facing, place the squares on the corners of the 11" blue squares and stitch along the crease as shown in Diagram 9. Trim and press.

3. Make 5 blocks as shown in Block 2 Diagram.

Assembling the Quilt

1. Join the blocks in 3 horizontal rows of 3 blocks each, alternating the blocks as shown in the photo. Pin and carefully sew all match points.

2. Join the rows to complete the quilt top.

Borders

1. See the general instructions on page 16 for tips on mitered border construction.

2. Stitch the borders to the quilt top, mitering the corners.

Quilting and Finishing

1. Mark the desired quilting designs on the quilt top. The quilt shown has outline quilting around the shapes, and meandering stitching in the blue background areas and in the border.

2. Layer backing, batting, and quilt top. Baste.

3. Quilt as desired.

4. Referring to the general instructions on page 21, make 166" of bias binding and apply to the quilt.

Diagram 8   Diagram 9   Block 2 Diagram

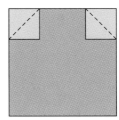 *Try Using a Novelty Print in This Quilt for a New Look*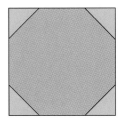

Wedding Star

Wedding Star by Mary Hickey, 1995, Keyport, Washington. Quilted by Hazel Montague.

This quilt has the same layout as *Cosmic Star*, but I used a novelty print in the Snowball blocks. Notice how one of the garden motifs is centered in each of those blocks. Select your novelty print first; then match the fabric for the star blocks to those colors.

Starry Path

Quilt: 37 ½" x 37 ½"
Finished Block Size: 9" square

Starry Path by Mary Hickey, 1994, Keyport, Washington. Quilted by Gretchen Engle.

Notice the placement of both color and value in this quilt. The areas
where the long, thin triangles meet the large half-square triangles appear to curve,
yet they are all sewn with straight seams.

Materials

1½ yards aqua print for background

½ yard turquoise leaf print for stars and centers of blocks

¾ yard navy stripe for stars and outer borders

⅛ yard magenta print for four-patches

¾ yard turquoise music print for half-square triangles and inner border

1¼ yards fabric for backing

1¼ yards batting

⅜ yard fabric for binding

Cutting

From the *aqua print*, cut:
• 3 (9" x 42") pieces.
• 2 (2" x 42") strips.

From the *turquoise leaf print*, cut:
• 1 (9" x 42") piece for star points.
• 1 (3½" x 42") strip. Cut strip into 9 (3½") squares for star centers.

From the *navy stripe*, cut:
• 1 (9" x 42") piece for star points.
• 4 (2¾" x 42") strips for outer border.

From the *magenta print*, cut:
• 2 (2" x 42") strips for four-patches.

From the *turquoise music print*, cut:
• 1 (9" x 42") piece for half-square triangles.
• 4 (3½" x 42") strips for inner borders.

Assembling the Blocks

1. Referring to the general instructions for making half-rectangle triangles on pages 137–138, use 1 each of the 9" x 42" pieces of aqua and leaf print to make 48 half-rectangle triangles (24 with turquoise on the right and 24 with the turquoise on the left) as follows:
• Cut the bias strips 2½".
• Cut the segments 3½".
• Cut the rectangles 2" x 3½".

2. Referring to the general instructions for making half-rectangle triangles on pages 137–138, use 1 each of the 9" x 42" pieces of aqua and navy to make 32 half-rectangle triangles (16 with navy on the right and 16 with navy on the left) as follows:

• Cut the bias strips 2½".
• Cut the segments 3½".
• Cut the rectangles 2" x 3½".

3. Join the star points together in pairs so that the sides with the background color are touching.

4. Referring to the general instructions for making half-square triangles on pages 55–56, use 1 each of the 9" x 42" piece of aqua and turquoise music print to make 16 (3½") half-square triangle units as follows:
• Cut the bias strips 3½".
• Cut the segments 3½".
• Cut the squares 3½".

5. Sew 1 (2" x 42") aqua strip to 1 magenta strip to make a strip set (Diagram 1). Repeat to make a second strip set.

6. Cut across the strip sets at 2" intervals as shown in Diagram 2 to make 40 segments.

7. Stitch the segments together as shown in Diagram 3 to make 20 four-patches.

8. Referring to the Block Assembly Diagrams, arrange the pieces for each block as shown. Make 5 of Block 1 and 4 of Block 2 as shown in Block Diagrams.

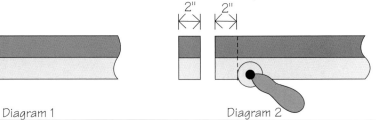

Diagram 1   Diagram 2

Diagram 3

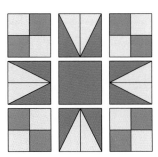

Block 1 Assembly Diagram

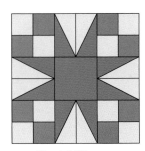

Block 1 Diagram

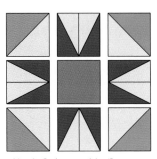

Block 2 Assembly Diagram

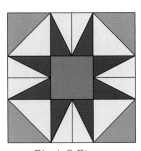

Block 2 Diagram

Assembling the Quilt

1. Join the blocks in 3 horizontal rows of 3 blocks each, alternating blocks as shown in *Quilt Top Assembly Diagram*. Pin and carefully sew all match points.
2. Join the rows to complete the quilt top.

Borders

1. Cut each of the 4 turquoise music-print inner border strips in half. Join 4 pairs of half-rectangle triangles together.
2. Sew the border strips together as shown in the *Quilt Top Assembly Diagram*, with a pair of half-rectangle triangles in the center.
3. Measure the length of the quilt top, measuring through the middle rather than along the sides. Keeping the pair of half-rectangle triangles in the center, trim 2 turquoise music-print border strips to this length. Stitch 1 of these to each side of the quilt, carefully matching the points.
4. Measure the width of the quilt top, measuring through the middle rather than along the sides. Keeping the pair of half-rectangle triangles in the center, trim 2 turquoise music-print border strips to this length. Stitch 1 of these each to the top and bottom of the quilt, carefully matching the points.
5. Measure the length of the quilt top, measuring through the middle rather than along the sides. Trim 2 navy stripe border strips to this length. Stitch 1 of these to each side of the quilt.
6. Measure the width of the quilt top, measuring through the middle rather than along the sides. Trim 2 navy stripe border strips to this length. Stitch 1 of these to the top and bottom of the quilt.

Quilting and Finishing

1. Mark the desired quilting designs on the quilt top. The quilt shown has outline quilting around the shapes and meandering stitching in the aqua background area.
2. Layer backing, batting, and quilt top. Baste.
3. Quilt as desired.
4. Referring to the general instructions on page 21, make 152" of bias binding and apply to the quilt.

Quilt Top Assembly Diagram

Garland Tulips

Quilt: 36" x 42"
Finished Block Size: 6" square

A vibrant red-and-green floral striped fabric sets the color scheme of this quilt.

Long, thin triangles create both the tulips and the leaves. Placing the

floral stripe between the block rows lends a garland effect to the quilt.

Materials

1 yard light print for background

¼ yard dark red print for tulips

¼ yard green print for leaves

⅛ yard or scraps red for tulip centers

1¼ yards floral stripe for vertical sashing and inner borders

⅜ yard dark green print for outer border

1¼ yards fabric for backing

1¼ yards batting

⅜ yard fabric for binding

Cutting

From the *light print*, cut:
- 2 (9" x 42") pieces.
- 5 (2" x 42") strips. From these:
  - Cut 2 of the strips into 15 (2" x 3½") pieces.
  - Cut 3 of the strips into 60 (2") squares.

From the *dark red print*, cut:
- 1 (9" x 42") piece.
- 1 (2" x 42") strip. Cut strip into 15 (2") squares for the base of each tulip.

From the *green print*, cut:
- 1 (9" x 42") piece for the leaves.

From the *red scraps*, cut:
- 15 (2") squares for the tulip centers.

From the *floral stripe*, cut:
- 2 (4½" x 42") strips for vertical sashing.
- 4 (4½" x 42") strips for inner border.

From the *dark green print*, cut:
- 4 (2¾" x 42") strips for outer border.

Assembling the Blocks

1. Referring to the general instructions for making half-rectangle triangles on pages 137–138, use 1 (9" x 42") piece each of the light print and dark red to make 30 half-rectangle triangles (15 with dark red on the right and 15 with dark red on the left) as follows:
- Cut the bias strips 2½".
- Cut the segments 3½".
- Cut the rectangles 2" x 3½".

2. Referring to the general instructions for making half-rectangle triangles on pages 137–138, use 1 (9" x 42") piece each of the light print and green to make 30 half-rectangle triangles (15 with green on the right and 15 with green on the left) as follows:
- Cut the bias strips 2½".
- Cut the segments 3½".
- Cut the rectangles 2" x 3½".

3. Referring to Diagram 1, arrange the red and background pieces as shown. Join pieces.

4. Referring to Diagram 2, arrange the green and background pieces as shown. Join pieces.

5. Referring to the Block Assembly Diagram, join the pieces to make 15 tulip blocks as shown.

Assembling the Quilt

1. Join the blocks in 3 vertical rows of 5 blocks each as shown in the Quilt Top Assembly Diagram. Pin and carefully sew match points.

2. Join block rows with floral stripe sashing strips as shown to complete quilt top.

Borders

1. See the general instructions on page 16 for tips on mitered border construction.

2. Stitch the borders to the quilt top, mitering corners.

Quilting and Finishing

1. Mark the desired quilting designs on the quilt top. The quilt shown has outline quilting around the tulip and leaf shapes, straight-line quilting on the edges of the floral stripes, and outline quilting around the flowers in the floral stripes.

2. Layer backing, batting, and quilt top. Baste.

3. Quilt as desired.

4. Referring to the general instructions on page 21, make 156" of bias binding and apply to the quilt.

Diagram 1   Diagram 2   Block Assembly Diagram

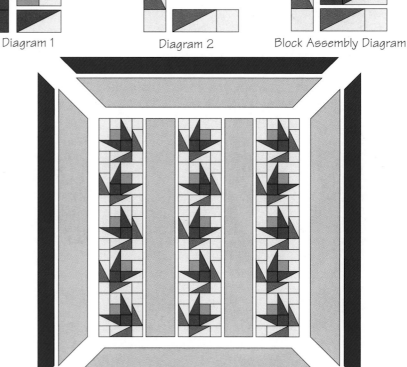

Quilt Top Assembly Diagram

Windblown Tulips, page 150.

Quilts Made with Appliqué

A lovely curved basket handle, a friendly heart, a festive tulip,
and a simple star are just a few of the countless motifs that can add softness to a
pieced block or become the focal point of an appliqué block. Here's a technique that
will make appliquéing these shapes easy and accurate.

Freezer-paper Appliqué

To make a smoothly curved edge on an appliqué shape, many quilters use a stiff paper template that forms a base around which the fabric is shaped. Many quilters like to use freezer paper (available in the canning supply sections of grocery stores) to cut templates. Freezer paper has a thin, shiny coating of plastic that softens and becomes sticky when heated with an iron. If the temperature of the iron is moderate, freezer paper can be pressed to the fabric temporarily.

1. Use a pencil to trace the appliqué shape on the dull (uncoated) side of the paper. Do not add seam allowances (Diagram 1).

2. Cut out the shape on the pencil line to create the template. If the shape you plan to appliqué is large, you may find it easier to work with stiffer paper. Try layering two pieces of freezer paper, shiny side against the dull side, and pressing them together. Pull the paper off your ironing board cover while it is still hot.

3. Use a warm, dry iron (permanent-press setting) to press the shiny (coated) side of the freezer-paper template to the wrong side of the appliqué fabric. Place the sharpest curves on the bias of the fabric (Diagram 2).

4. Cut the fabric around the freezer paper, leaving a narrow ⅛" to ³⁄₁₆" seam allowance (Diagram 3).

5. Using a glue stick, spread a small amount of glue around the outer edges

of the paper (Diagram 4).

6. Use your fingernail or a toothpick to fold the edges of the fabric around the edges of the paper (Diagram 5).

7. Baste the shapes in position on the quilt block (Diagram 6).

8. Use a blindstitch to appliqué the shapes in place (Diagram 7).

9. Working from the back of the quilt block, carefully snip the background fabric open behind each shape and pull out the paper (Diagram 8). Trim excess fabric, if desired, leaving a ⅛" seam allowance.

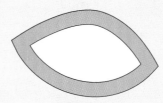
Diagram 1

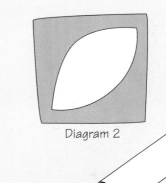
Diagram 2

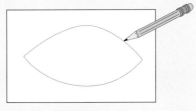
Diagram 3

Diagram 4

Diagram 5

Diagram 6

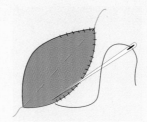
Diagram 7

Diagram 8

Windblown Tulips

Quilt: 50" x 50"
Finished Block Size: 7" square

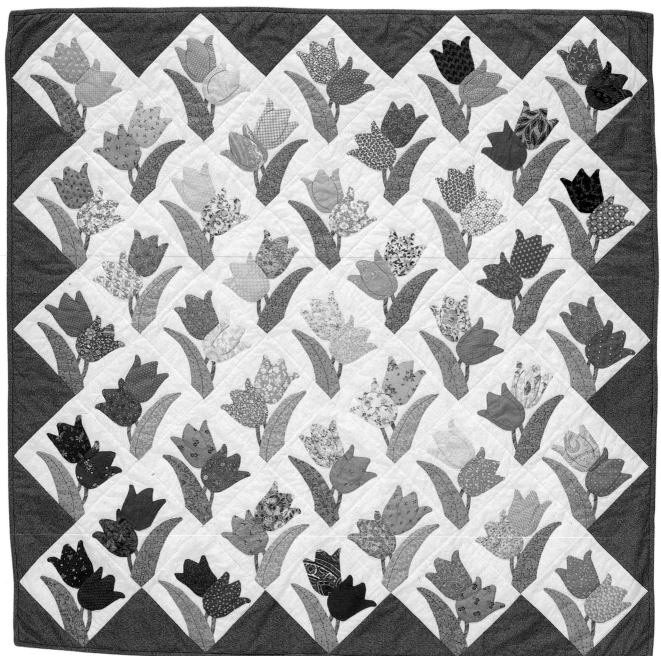

Windblown Tulips by Carolann Palmer, 1994, Seattle, Washington.

Old-fashioned blocks sewn with 1930s-style scraps make this a wonderful

handwork project. The colors of tulips gradually change from dark to light and from

color to color, creating order and energy at the same time.

Materials

2¼ yards white for background

¼ yard each of 3 different greens for leaves and stems

1 yard green for side and corner triangles

Scraps of lavender, purple, yellow, gold, red, and pink for the tulips

2 yards fabric for backing

1½ yards 60"-wide batting

½ yard fabric for binding

Cutting

Refer to the general instructions for appliqué on page 149. Patterns are on page 152.

From the *white,* cut:

• 41 (7½") background squares.

From the *greens,* cut:

• 41 short stems (Template 1).

• 41 long stems (Template 2).

• 41 leaves (Template 5). *Note:* In our sample, the leaves are blowing both left and right. To achieve this effect, cut 25 of the leaves with the template face up and 16 with the template face down.

From the *green for side and corner triangles,* cut:

• 4 (11¼") squares. Cut the squares in quarters diagonally to make 16 side setting triangles.

• 2 (6") squares. Cut the squares in half diagonally to make 4 corner triangles.

From the *scraps of lavender, purple, yellow, gold, red, and pink,* cut:

• 41 tulips (Template 3).

• 41 tulips (Template 4).

Note: Each block has a pair of tulips in different shades of the same color. The quilt shown has 9 pairs of red tulips, 7 pairs of pink tulips, 9 pairs of yellow/gold tulips, 7 pairs of lavender tulips, and 9 pairs of purple tulips.

Assembling the Blocks

Referring to the photo and to the *Appliqué Placement Diagram* **on page** 152, appliqué the stems, tulips, and leaves in numerical order as shown. Make 16 blocks as shown in the diagram and 25 mirror-image blocks.

Assembling the Quilt

1. Referring to the photo and the *Quilt Top Assembly Diagram,* arrange the blocks and setting pieces in diagonal rows in a graded color arrangement.

2. Join the blocks in diagonal rows.

3. Join the rows to complete the quilt top.

Quilting and Finishing

1. Mark the desired quilting designs on the quilt top. The quilt shown has outline quilting around the tulips, stems, and leaves, and around each block. The quilting lines on the tulips and leaves are indicated on the Appliqué Placement Diagram.

2. Layer backing, batting, and quilt top. Baste.

3. Quilt as desired.

4. Referring to the general instructions on page 21, make 200" of bias binding and apply to the quilt.

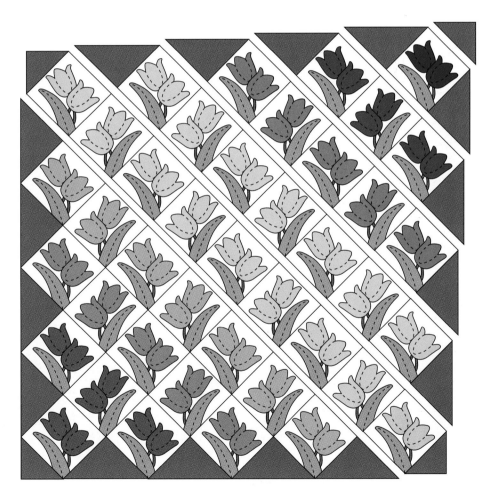

Quilt Top Assembly Diagram

Appliqué Placement Diagram and Finished-size Patterns
(Dashed lines indicate quilting lines.)

Buttoned Hearts and Stars

Quilt: 22½" x 28"
Finished Block Size: 5½"

Buttoned Hearts and Stars by Mary Hickey, 1995, Keyport, Washington.

Blanket stitching and buttons are in keeping with the folk-art theme of this little quilt.

You can work the blanket stitch by hand or by machine—just be sure to use

a black or contrasting thread to show off the decorative stitching.

Materials

½ yard or scraps of 8–12 different tans for backgrounds

¼ yard or scraps of red for hearts and borders

¼ yard or scraps of blue for hearts and borders

¼ yard or scraps of green for hearts and border

¼ yard or scraps of gold for stars and border

1 yard of paper-backed fusible web

⅞ yard fabric for backing

⅞ yard batting

½ yard fabric for bias binding

20 red buttons

20 blue buttons

20 green buttons

20 gold-and-rust buttons

Black embroidery floss

Cutting

From the *tans*, cut:

• 12 (6") squares for backgrounds.

From each piece of *colored fabric*, cut:

• 3 (5") squares for appliqué shapes.

From the *paper-backed fusible web*, cut:

• 12 (5") squares. Trace 2 of Template 1, 7 of Template 2, and 3 of Template 3 onto the paper side. Follow the manufacturer's instructions to fuse the paper to the wrong side of the colored squares. Cut out the heart and star shapes along the drawn lines. Remove the paper backing.

From the *red*, cut:

• 1 (3¼" x 36") strip for the top border.

• 1 (3¼") square for the lower left border corner.

From the *blue*, cut:

• 1 (3¼" x 36") strip for the right side border.

• 1 (3¼") square for the upper left border corner.

From the *green*, cut:

• 1 (3¼" x 36") strip for the left side border.

• 1 (3¼") square for the lower right border corner.

From the *gold*, cut:

• 1 (3¼" x 36") strip for the bottom border.

• 1 (3¼") square for the upper right border corner.

Assembling the Blocks

1. Follow the manufacturer's instructions to fuse the appliqué shapes to the tan background squares.

Tip: Add visual interest to your quilt by tilting the appliqué shapes in different directions, as shown in the photo.

2. Use 2 strands of the black embroidery floss to blanket-stitch around each shape (Blanket Stitch Diagram).

Tip: Some sewing machines have a blanket-stitch option among their many fancy stitches. Or, if you want a really speedy alternative, try using a permanent fine-line fabric pen to "pen-stitch" the blanket-stitch outline.

Assembling the Quilt

1. Referring to the *Quilt Top Assembly Diagram*, join the blocks in 4 horizontal rows of 3 blocks each.

2. Join the rows to complete the quilt top.

Borders

1. Measure the length of the quilt, measuring through the middle rather than along the sides. Trim the green and blue border strips to this length. Stitch these to the sides of the quilt.

2. Measure the width of the quilt (excluding borders), measuring through the middle rather than along the ends. Trim the red and gold border strips to this length. Join the border corner squares to the ends of each strip, as shown in the *Quilt Top Assembly Diagram*. Stitch these to the top and bottom of the quilt.

Quilt Top Assembly Diagram

Quilting and Finishing

1. Mark the desired quilting designs on the quilt top. The quilt shown has outline quilting around the blocks, groups of 3 diagonal lines through the corners of each block, and a curved design in the borders.

2. Layer backing, batting, and quilt top. Baste.

3. Quilt as desired.

4. Using the photo as a guide, arrange the buttons as desired. Use cellophane tape to secure them in place temporarily. Hand- or machine-sew the buttons to the quilt top.

5. Referring to the general instructions on page 21, make 125" of bias binding and apply to the quilt.

Blanket Stitch Diagram

3

2

1

Twinkle, Twinkle

Quilt: 19" x 19"

Who can resist a chubby star, especially when it has its own plump heart?

Stitch your little stars and then machine-quilt

your tiny masterpiece in a meandering design with metallic thread.

Materials

⅜ yard white for background

¼ yard blue star print for stars and outer border

¼ yard red for hearts and inner border

¼ yard fabric for binding

Cutting

From *white,* cut:

• 1 (13") square for background.

From *blue star print,* cut:

• 9 (4") squares for stars.

• 4 (3½" x 21") strips for outer border.

From *red,* cut:

• 9 (2") squares for hearts.

• 4 (1" x 21") strips for inner border.

Assembling the Quilt

1. Divide the white square into 9 spaces, each 4" square.

2. Referring to the general instructions for appliqué on page 149 and using the patterns at right, cut 9 blue stars and 9 red hearts.

3. Center 1 star in each space.

4. Appliqué stars.

5. Appliqué a heart in the middle of each star.

6. Trim white square to 12½".

Borders

1. Measure the length of the quilt top, measuring through the middle rather than along the sides. Trim 2 red inner border strips to this length. Stitch 1 of these to each side of quilt *(Quilt Top Assembly Diagram).*

2. Measure the width of the quilt top, measuring through the middle rather than along the sides. Trim 2 red inner border strips to this length. Stitch 1 to the top and bottom of the quilt.

3. Measure the length of the quilt top, measuring through the middle rather than along the sides. Trim 2 blue star print outer border strips to this length. Stitch 1 of these to each side of quilt.

4. Measure the width of the quilt top, measuring through the middle rather than along the sides. Trim 2 blue star print outer border strips to this length. Stitch 1 of these to the top and bottom of the quilt.

Quilting and Finishing

1. Mark desired quilting designs on the quilt top. The quilt shown has outline quilting around the stars and meandering stitching in silver thread in the background.

2. Layer backing, batting, and quilt top. Baste.

3. Quilt as desired.

4. Referring to the general instructions on page 21, make 76" of bias binding and apply to the quilt.

Quilt Top Assembly Diagram

Star

Heart

Straw Hat

Quilt: 26" x 26"

Straw Hat by Cleo Nollette, 1995, Seattle, Washington.

Cleo Nollette used both sides of a checked tan fabric to create the
straw hat on this quilt. A jaunty bow and a sprig of primrose add the
finishing touches to this fine spring bonnet.

Materials

¾ yard blue-and-white stripe for background
¼ yard tan check for hat
¼ yard rose for flower and inner border
¼ yard blue floral print for outer border
Scraps of blue for ribbon
Scrap of green for leaves
Scrap of pink for flower center
¾ yard fabric for backing
¾ yard batting
¼ yard fabric for binding

Cutting

Refer to the general instructions for appliqué on page 149. Patterns are on page 160.
From the *blue-and-white stripe*, cut:
• 1 (18½") square for background.
From the *wrong side of tan check*, cut:
• the brim of the hat (Template 1).
From the *right side of tan check*, cut:
• the crown of the hat (Template 2).
From the *blue scraps*, cut:
• 1 hatband (Template 3).
• 2 bows (Templates 4 and 5).
• 2 ribbons (Templates 6 and 7).
From the *scrap of green*, cut:
• 3 leaves (Templates 8, 9, and 10).
From the *rose*, cut:
• 5 petals for the flower (Template 11).
• 4 (1¼" x 36") strips for inner border.
From the *pink*, cut:
• 1 flower center (Template 12).
From the *blue floral print*, cut:
• 4 (3½" x 36") strips for outer border.

Assembling the Quilt

Referring to the Appliqué Placement Diagram, appliqué the shapes to the background in numerical order.

Borders

1. Measure the length of the quilt top, measuring through the middle rather than along the sides. Trim 2 red inner border strips to this length. Stitch 1 of these to each side of the quilt.
2. Measure the width of the quilt top, measuring through the middle rather than along the sides. Trim 2 red inner border strips to this length. Stitch 1 of these to the top and bottom of the quilt.
3. Measure the length of the quilt top, measuring through the middle rather than along the sides. Trim 2 blue floral print outer border strips to this length. Stitch 1 of these to each side of the quilt.
4. Measure the width of the quilt top, measuring through the middle rather than along the sides. Trim 2 blue floral print outer border strips to this length.

Stitch 1 of these to the top and bottom of the quilt.

Quilting and Finishing

1. Mark the desired quilting designs on the quilt top. The quilt shown has straight-line quilting on the stripes and outline quilting around the hat, ribbon, flower, and leaves. The border is quilted with a curved design.
2. Layer backing, batting, and quilt top. Baste.
3. Quilt as desired.
4. Referring to the general instructions on page 21, make 104" of bias binding and apply to the quilt.

Appliqué Placement Diagram

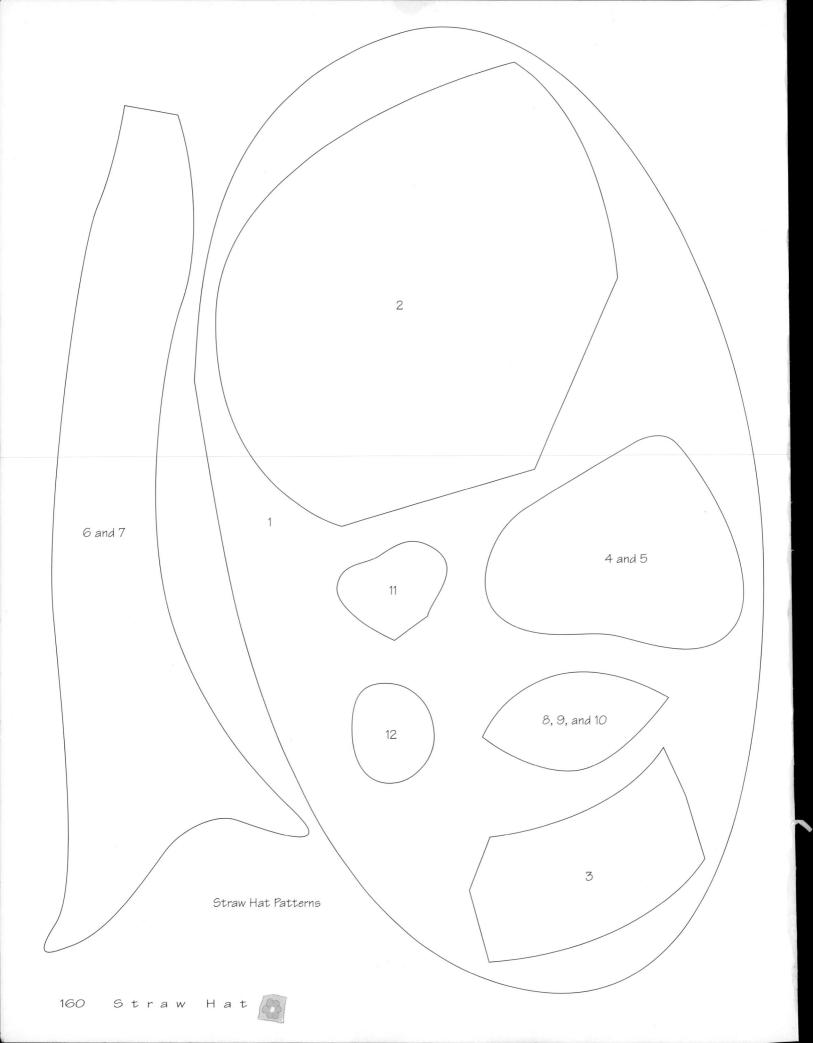

6 and 7

2

1

11

4 and 5

12

8, 9, and 10

3

Straw Hat Patterns